Little Genius Brain Boosting Activity Book

An imprint of Om Books International

Om Books International

Reprinted in 2025

Corporate & Editorial Office
A-12, Sector 64, Noida 201 301
Uttar Pradesh, India
Phone: +91 120 477 4100
Email: editorial@ombooks.com
Website: www.ombooksinternational.com

Sales Office
107, Ansari Road, Darya Ganj
New Delhi 110 002, India
Phone: +91 11 4000 9000
Email: sales@ombooks.com
Website: www.ombooks.com

ISBN: 978-93-5276-640-6

Printed in India

10 9 8 7 6 5 4 3 2

Contents

WHO AM I?

Help the Vocabird learn new words by matching the pictures to the correct words.

SPELL CHECK

Unscramble the letters and fill in the blanks with the names of the pictures given below.

cihckne

chicken

sepgra

____

sehroeas

____

eykhoc

____

erlfow

____

dcotor

____

CONSO-HUNT

Look at the pictures and fill in the blanks with the correct consonants.

PICTURE PERFECT

Look at the pictures. Spell their names and complete the crossword on the next page for the Vocabirds.

PICTURE PERFECT

BLENDED CODES

Colour the petals according to the consonant blends written on them. The colour code is given below.

Voca tip: A consonant blend is a mix of consonant sounds in a word. For example: "pl" in play.

pl sn br tr cl

FUN WITH DIGRAPHS

Look at the pictures. Tick the picture whose name has a consonant digraph.

Voca tip: When two consonants create one sound in a word, we call it a digraph. For example, ch, sh, th, nd and wh.

EUREKA!

Make new words from the digraphs and blends given in the centre.

RHYME TIME

Read the first word and circle its rhyming word in each row.

Voca tip: Rhyming words have similar sounds.

bear	sit	ship	care	but
red	bed	tile	tear	touch
tough	teach	seek	big	rough
right	bat	left	might	small
late	kit	gate	fight	rail
blue	true	skit	tick	car
niece	stand	run	which	peace
check	cold	blue	deck	tan
know	grow	wet	bye	ring

RHYMTASTIC

Read the poem carefully and list the rhyming words in it.

The Squirrel

Teeny, tiny,
Hippity hop,
Up he goes,
To the tree top!

Whirly, twirly,
Round and round,
Down he scampers,
To the ground.

Furly, curly,
What a tail!
Tall as a feather,
Broad as a snail!

Where's his supper?
In the shell.
Snap, crack,
Out it fell.

PERFECT PAIRS

Match the male animals to their female partners.

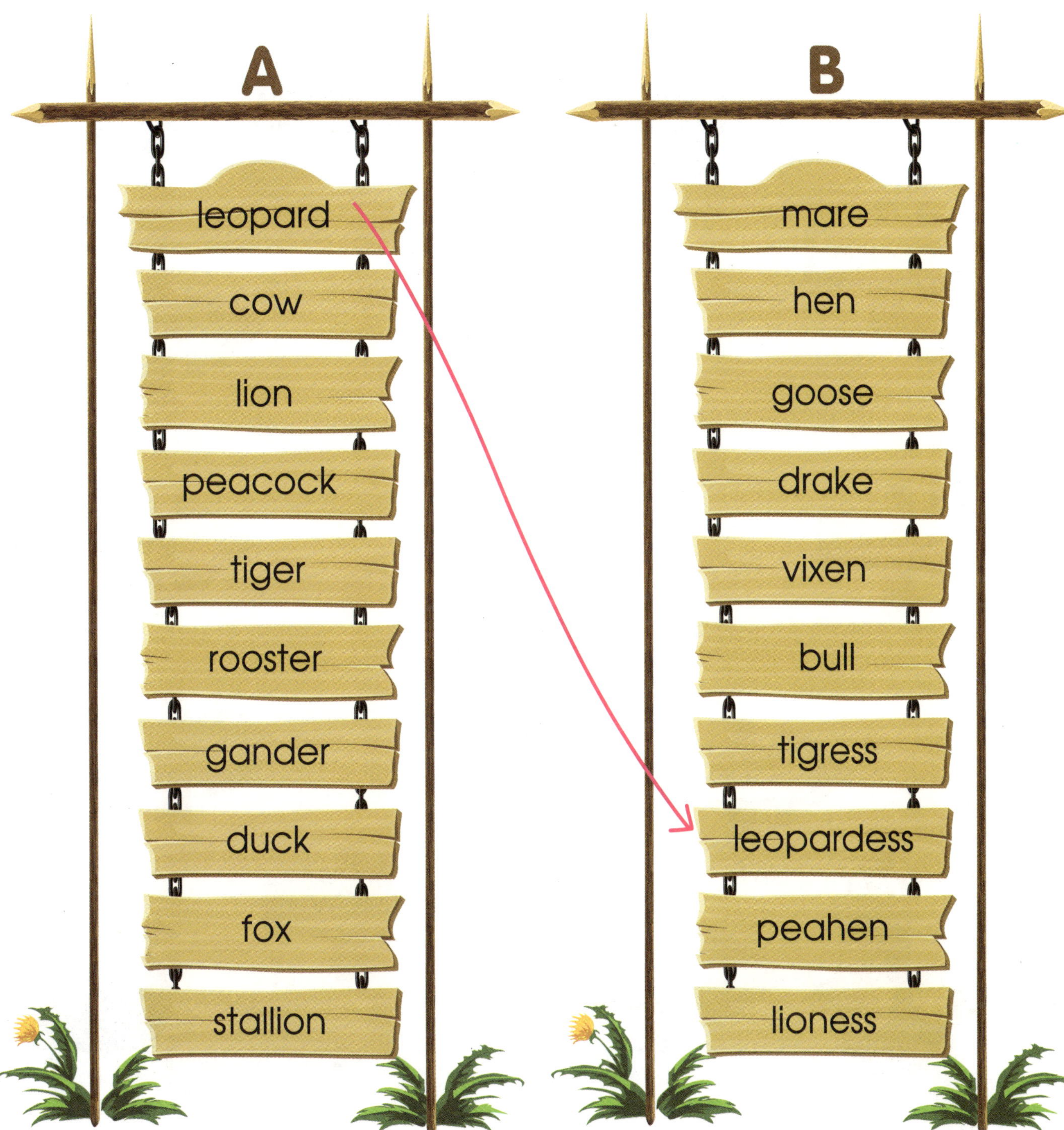

FIND MY FRIENDS

Help the Vocabird find his friends by colouring the path with his female friends pink and his male friends blue. The starting points are given to you.

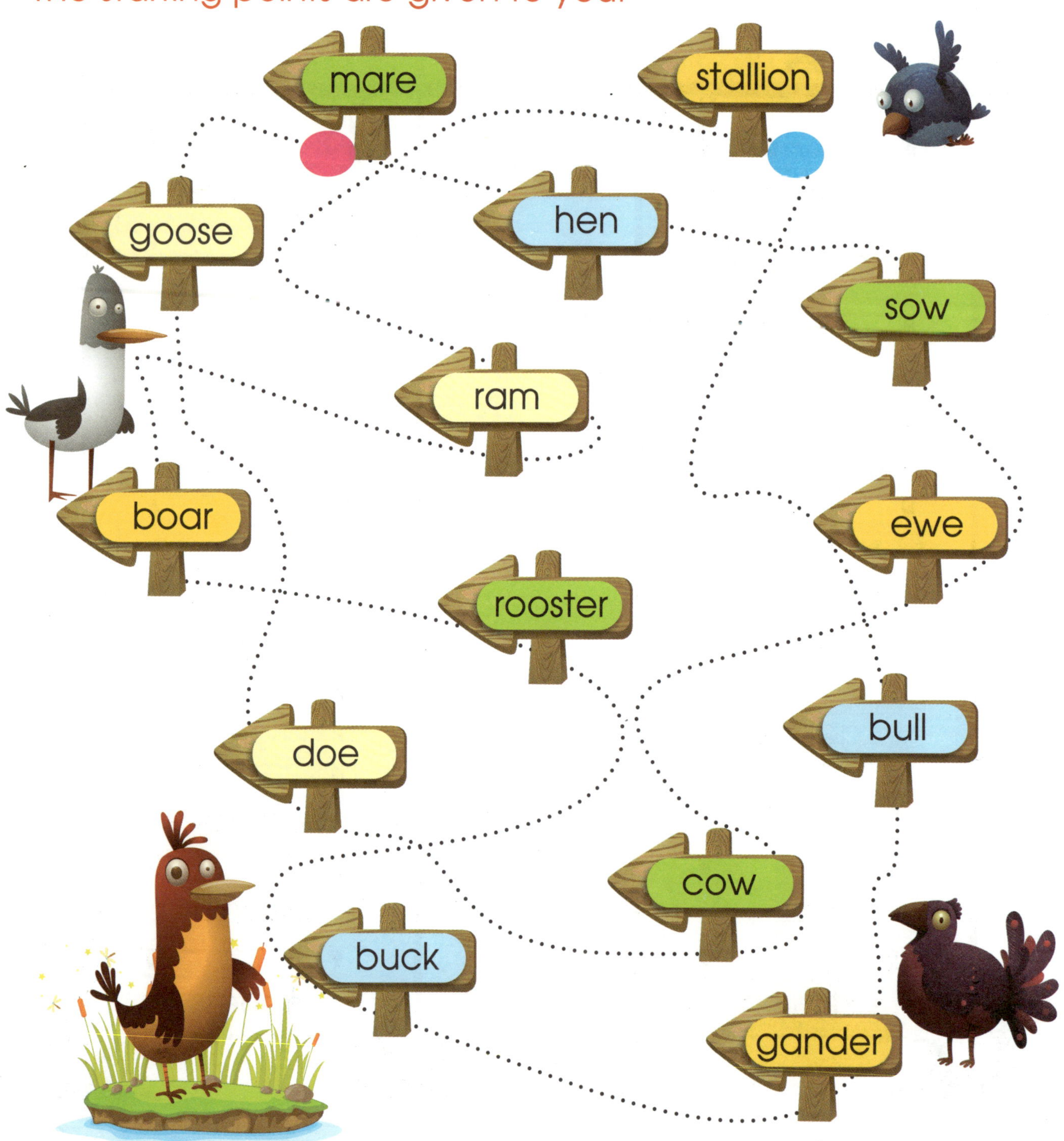

WHERE'S EVERYONE?

Help the Vocabird spot and circle different animal habitats in the puzzle given below.

HOME SWEET HOME

Fill in the blanks to help the Vocabird learn about animals and their habitats.

live in deserts	live in oceans	live on farms
live in extreme cold climates	live in forests	live with people

1) Domestic animals - live with people.

2) Ocean animals - ______________________.

3) Forest animals - ______________________.

4) Desert animals - ______________________.

5) Farm animals - ______________________.

6) Polar animals - ______________________.

GOING HOME

Match the animals to their habitats.

forest | desert | ocean | wetlands | farm

HOMELY MATCH

Match the houses to their names.

PINK OR BLUE?

Colour the circle below the female gender with a pink crayon and the male gender with a blue crayon.

WE ARE FAMILY

Look at the family picture and help the Vocabird fill in the blanks.

John

Peggy

Myra

Ron

Dan

Jenny

Ashton

Grandfather's name – John

Grandmother's name – __________

Father's name – __________

Mother's name – __________

Sister's name – __________

Brother's name – __________

Baby's name – __________

HOUSE HUNTING

Fill in the blanks using the words given at the bottom of the page.

1) Places with very little rainfall have flat roof houses.

2) People who travel a lot live in a ______________ , which helps them to move around easily.

3) Places with heavy rainfall have ______________.

4) Eskimos live in an ______________.

5) Houses with eight sides are called ______________.

6) The Queen of England lives in a ______________.

7) A ______________ house is made of wood.

8) A house made from natural materials is known as ______________.

VEHICLE WOES

Help the Vocabird identify the vehicles and fill in the blanks with the correct letters.

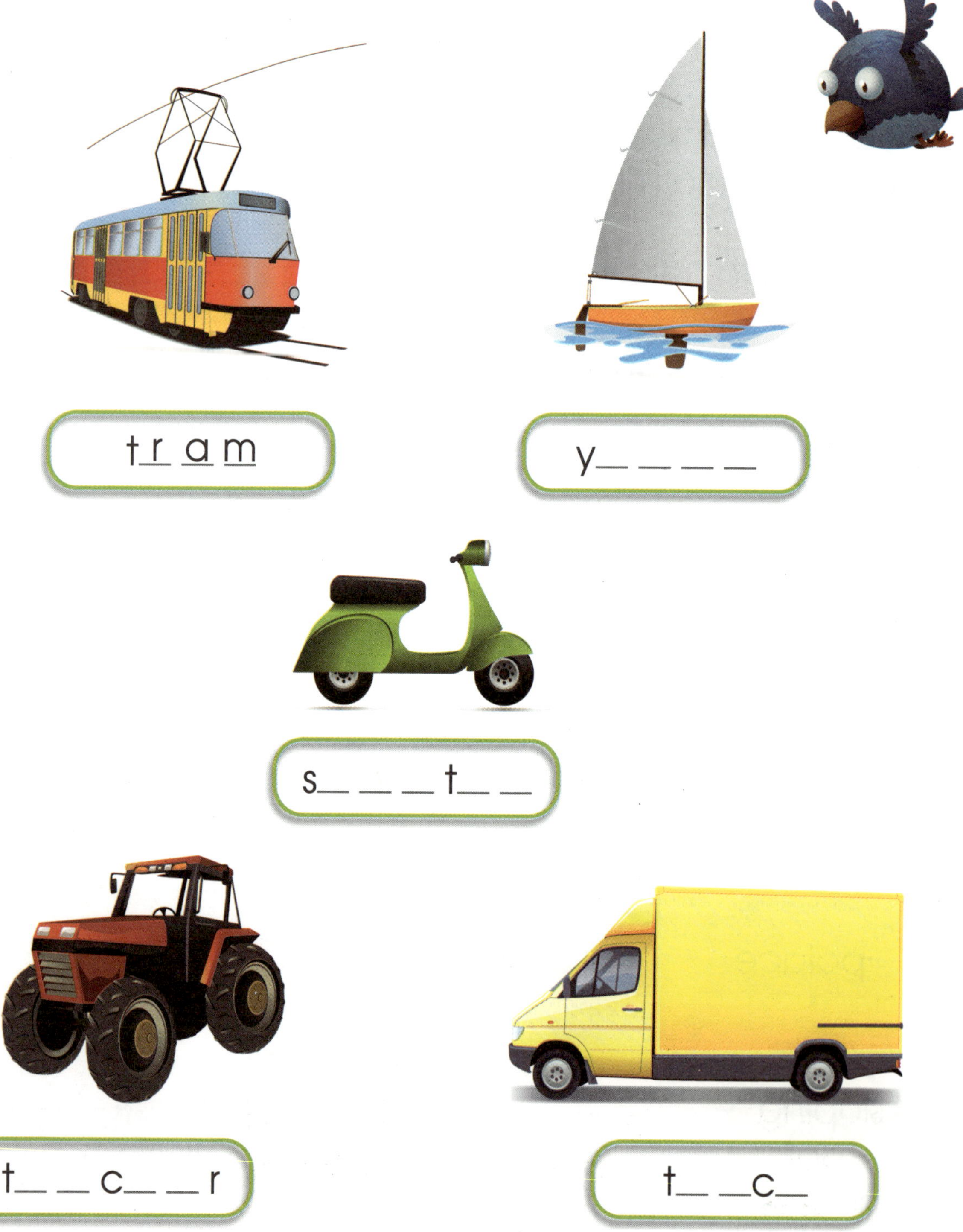

TRAVEL BUDDIES

Write "land", "water" or "air" under each mode of transport.

Voca tip: Some vehicles travel on land, some vehicles sail in water and some fly in the air.

USEFUL UTILITIES

Fill in the blanks with the correct option.

1) We fill water in the ____jug____.

home | jug | hand

2) We open the __________ to get fresh air.

basket | pan | window

3) We unlock the door with a __________.

key | apple | toes

4) We use a __________ to cut vegetables.

light | bulb | knife

5) At night, we switch on the __________ to see clearly.

fan | car | tube light

6) People keep a __________ under their head before going to sleep.

fan | pillow | nose

HOUSEHOLD HUNT

Circle the household items from the pictures given below.

OPPOSITES ATTRACT

Look at the words given below and draw a star below the pair of antonyms for the Vocabird.

MATCH MAKING

Help the Vocabird connect the words to their synonyms.

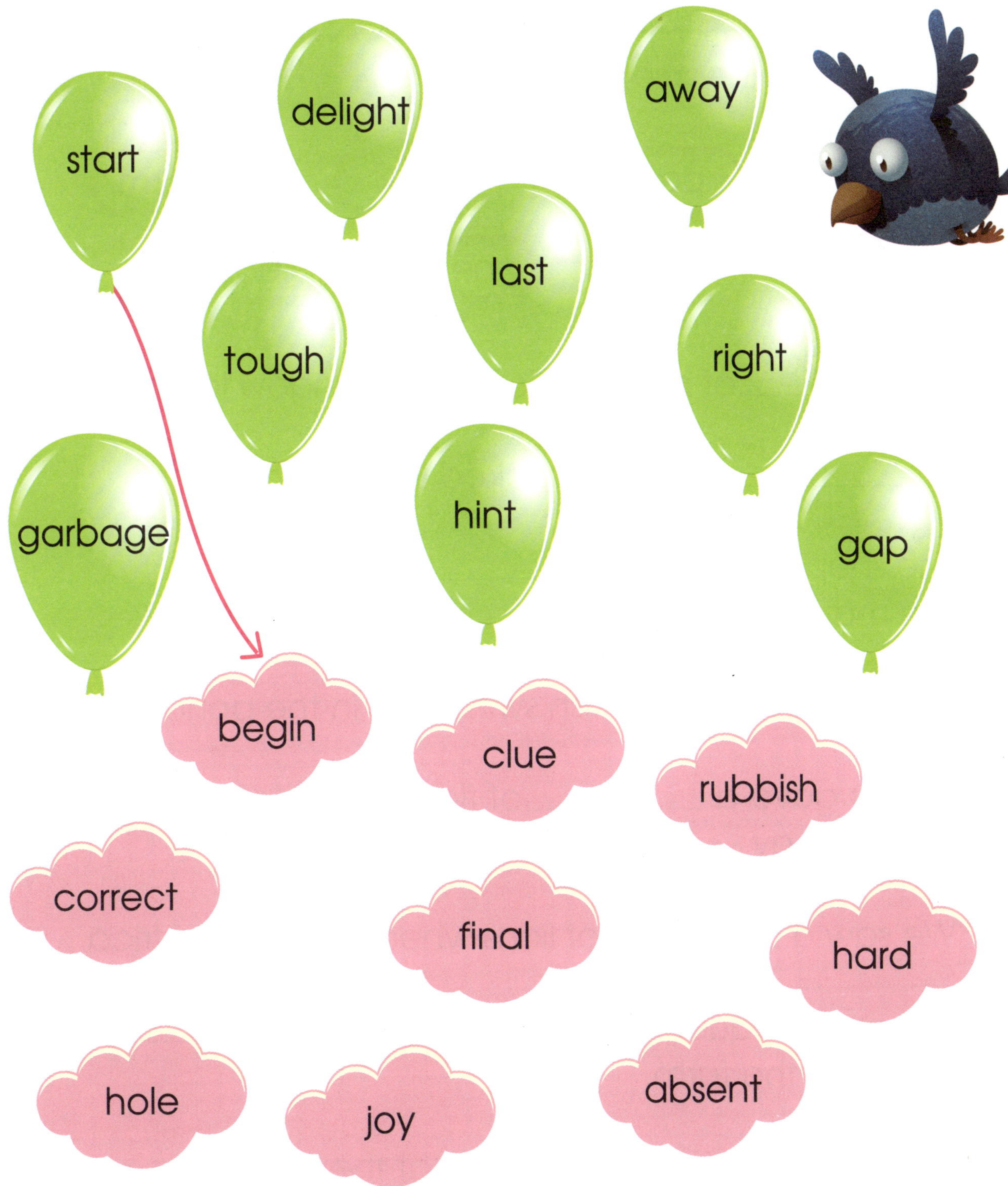

COLLECTIVE CHOICES

Fill in the blanks with collective nouns.

Voca tip: Collective nouns are words which represent a group of things, people, etc.

gaggle pack flock swarm
pride school herd bouquet

1) A ___flock___ of birds flew out of his window last night.

2) A __________ of bees attacked Farmer Jones.

3) The shepherd led his __________ of sheep up the mountain.

4) I saw a __________ of fish swimming in the pond.

5) Father gave a __________ of flowers to Mother on her birthday.

6) We saw a __________ of lions when we visited Africa.

7) The endless quacking came from the __________ of geese at the farm.

8) A __________ of wolves howled at the full moon.

SPOT 'EM ALL

This Vocabird is looking for common nouns. Spot and circle them from the words given below.

Voca tip: Common nouns are a common name given to a group of things, animals, etc.

GETTING PICKY

Sort the words given below in the correct columns.

student | problem | bunch | year

flight | flock | hand | troop

band | system

Collective Nouns
flock

Common Nouns
student

SCRAMBLE HUNT

Unscramble the words in the clue boxes. Spot and circle them in the grid below.

grnee	lalh	rma	bena	etki
sudt	sewt	ckpa	aceg	locud

q	s	g	r	e	e	n	e	w	x
d	u	s	t	r	w	e	s	t	c
x	d	x	o	h	l	m	w	h	l
n	b	e	a	n	j	e	n	a	o
v	t	v	r	t	c	v	o	l	u
b	p	a	c	k	a	p	c	l	d
n	j	w	d	c	g	n	a	k	l
m	k	i	t	e	e	b	r	m	b
l	l	n	f	s	f	s	m	e	s
g	f	g	h	f	z	t	d	i	h

SENTENCE SCRAMBLE

Happy the Hippo has messed up his sentences! Tick the ones that make sense and cross out the ones that don't.

Cuckoos sweet sing. ☐

Mary has a little lamb. ☐

I going to are the zoo. ☐

I will feed my cat. ☐

My animal favourite are dog. ☐

Camels are usually found in deserts. ☐

Is the monkey eating a banana? ☐

NAME SORTING

Help Tickles the Tiger sort out the nouns from these sentences in the correct column.

A herd of cattle is passing by.

Mojo the monkey is looking at me.

Elephants are the largest animals on land.

We named our dog Lucy.

The Gir forest has lions.

Have you seen that litter of kittens?

The hyena's laughter was scary.

Proper	Common	Abstract	Collective

Help Bingo the Bear underline two countable nouns in **BLUE** and two uncountable nouns in **RED**.

Once upon a time, there lived a family of three bears in the woods. They were Mama Bear, Papa Bear and Baby Bear. One day, they went out for a walk. Mama Bear cooked up some delicious porridge before they left.

While they were gone, a little girl named Goldilocks walked by their house. She smelt the porridge and her tummy began to rumble. She went in and saw three bowls on the table.

She ran towards them and took a spoonful of Papa Bear's porridge. But it was too hot. Then, she grabbed a spoonful of Mama Bear's porridge. But it was too cold. Finally, she tried Baby Bear's porridge. It was just right! She ate it all up hungrily.

After a while, she felt sleepy. She spotted Papa Bear's bed, but it was too hard. She lay down on Mama Bear's bed, but it was too soft. Finally, she tried Baby Bear's bed, which was just right. She jumped onto the bed and fell asleep in a jiffy!

Soon, the bears returned home. Baby Bear started crying when he saw his porridge bowl empty. "Somebody ate all my porridge!" He cried and ran to his room. And what did he see there? A strange little girl fast asleep on his bed! Baby bear screamed loudly. Goldilocks woke up. She was shocked to see three angry bears at the foot of the bed. She jumped out and ran away as fast as she could.

Let's help Laurie the Lion circle the subjects and underline the predicates in the sentences below.

Singing birds make us happy.

A camel is called the ship of the desert.

Forests have a varlety of trees.

Cows give us milk.

Wild animals live in jungles.

Dogs are a man's best friend.

SOUND ALOUD

Help Hagrid the Hippo choose the correct homophones to complete the sentence.

A horse is ______, whereas a mare is female.

a. mail b. male

There are ______ many bees in this forest.

a. too b. two

We saw a ______ on our hiking trip.

a. deer b. dear

Did you ______ the sound of the bear?

a. here b. hear

The cat is ______ favourite pet.

a. their b. there

The ______ lost the race.

a. hair b. hare

ARTICLE TRACKER

Leo the Leopard wrote a poem but forgot to add articles.
Can you add articles in the correct places?

Once there was ________ cute little leopard,
But he didn't want to be cute,
He wanted to be __________ shepherd!

What he loved most was to keep
__________ close, watchful eye,
On those naughty little sheep.

He liked to watch them graze all day,
Then lead them back home
For __________ good night's stay.

But the sheep didn't like
__________ leopard too much,
They were afraid of his sharp touch.

When they saw __________ leopard coming by,
They ran as fast
As their little feet could try.

__________ leopard was sad, but what could he do,
He gave up being __________ shepherd,
And went to __________ zoo!

Verbie the Worm wants you to circle all the verbs in these sentences and connect them to his basket.

The hungry lion is roaring.

The owl is hiding because it is daytime.

The crow is flying down to steal the cheese.

Goldilocks fell asleep on baby bear's bed.

The animals are drinking water from the stream.

Why is your dog walking like that?

She took her cat to the vet.

All his friends thanked the bear.

The crafty fox hides behind that bush every day.

A tiny mouse lived under the hole.

TIGER TENSE

Help Timmy the Tiger name the tense of the underlined words. Write whether they are present, past or future tense on the blanks below.

The bird is flying high up in the sky.

____

I will take my dog for a walk shortly.

____

The boy saw how the elephant was being bathed.

____

The cat rolled in the sand and got dirty.

____

My pet dog is drinking milk this morning.

____

Ronnie the Rhino is on an adjective quest. Spot and circle all the adjectives in the grid.

s	l	e	b	s	l	e	p	o	n	g
w	q	f	e	r	o	c	t	g	r	u
i	w	b	a	i	w	k	m	r	u	m
m	f	e	r	o	c	i	o	u	s	p
g	r	a	c	e	f	u	l	m	c	g
i	w	u	i	i	w	k	m	p	a	m
m	e	t	p	r	e	t	t	y	r	p
m	h	i	u	m	s	l	i	m	y	g
i	w	f	l	d	h	i	l	a	z	y
n	z	u	n	n	y	k	n	z	a	n
s	h	l	g	g	p	u	w	i	l	d

Read the sentences and help Jenny the Giraffe decide whether they have adjectives of quality or quantity.

The dog has two puppies. ______________

The giraffe is a tall animal. ______________

The crafty fox wanted the cheese. ______________

Some birds cannot fly. ______________

There are many species of animals, birds and insects to be found. ______________

Elephants have long trunks. ______________

Dinosaurs are extinct animals. ______________

Arnie the Ant wants to fill up the jungle with adverbs. Help him add the correct ones to these sentences first!

Hyenas laugh ________________.

A cat can catch a mouse ________________.

Cheetahs run ________________.

We ________________ go trekking in the forest.

The little bird sang ________________.

often

loudly

joyfully

quickly

easily

Builder Beaver is constructing a gender chart. Can you help him fill in the correct words?

If a cow is female, a male is a ________.

If a tigress is female, a male is a ________.

If a lioness is female, a male is a ________.

If a mare is female, a male is a ________.

If a hen is female, a male is a ________.

COUNT AND MATCH

Match these singular animals to their plural forms.

macaw	squirrels
squirrel	rhinoceroses
rhinoceros	mongooses
mongoose	macaws

Help Oliver the Owl understand synonyms and antonyms. Read the sentences. Mark the synonyms with 'S' and the antonyms with 'A' in the boxes alongside.

Sentence	Word	Box	Word	Box
This is a dense forest.	crammed	☐	clear	☐
Wild beasts inhabit the forest.	mild	☐	untamed	☐
Pretty flowers grow amidst the trees.	beautiful	☐	repulsive	☐
Our ecology needs to be preserved.	destroyed	☐	conserved	☐
The berries that grow here are delicious.	nasty	☐	tasty	☐
A clear stream is flowing here.	murky	☐	clean	☐
The antelope has big horns.	small	☐	large	☐

PICKING PRONOUNS

Pinto the Parrot needs to pick out the correct pronouns to complete these sentences. Can you help him?

(I / She) like animals.

Jack and (I / me) are watching a movie about bears.

(That / These) puppy needs water.

Dolly likes turtles. (She / He) has got one as a pet.

Mary told (me / I) an interesting story about elephants.

LEAFY LINKS

Choose the correct word from the flowers to complete the sentences below.

There are clouds ______ the sky.

The sun is shining from ______ the clouds.

The giraffe is walking ______ the elephant.

Can you see that bird ______ the two trees?

The crocodile is swimming ______ the river.

We can see fish swimming ______ the water.

The woodpecker vanished ______ its nest.

Flowers are growing ______ those trees.

The monkey is swinging ______ tree to tree.

The shepherd is sitting ______ his sheep.

in from behind near

under beside between across

Join and rewrite the following sentences using a preposition from the flowers.

The fox wanted the cheese. He flattered the crow.

____

The turtle didn't give up. He was slow.

____

No one came to help the shepherd. He had cried wolf many times.

____

____

The ant did not help the grasshopper. He was lazy.

____

The stork ate her dinner. The fox watched.

____

ERROR SPOTTER

Spot and circle the errors in the sentences below.

Where I can find a pet shop?

We have visited Ranthambore sanctuary last weekend.

The woman which works as forest officer is from my city.

Although it was raining but we had the hike.

I look forward to meet my friends outside the woods.

Every animals likes freedom.

Spot and circle the interjections from the pebbles below.

Ouch

Water

Phew

Book

Hey

Yikes

Oh no

Grammar

Wow

Coffee

Turtle

Soup

PROVERB PROBLEMS

Mojo the Monkey messed up all these proverbs! Rearrange the words in the correct order to make meaningful proverbs.

change leopard spots cannot A its

____

silk monkey monkey less no A is a in

____

rotten barrel A spoils apple the

____

An snared old easily fox not is

____

paints A picture words thousand a

____

The worm the early catches bird

____

can lead can't a drink horse to,
you make You but water him

____

____

INSPECTOR IDIOM

Help Inspector Eagle spot and circle the idioms in these sentences.

Please be clear, do not beat around the bush.

Trying to learn karate like this is not right,
you are barking up the wrong tree.

Let someone else hear that cock and bull story.

Cry wolf, and you are sure to learn your lesson.

The first ranker turned out to be a dark horse.

Don't count your chickens before they hatch.

Hold your horses, hard work always pays.

Help these animals spell their name correctly by filling the blanks with the correct letters.

Rhino _ _ ros

Hippopo _ _ mus

T _ _ can

M _ _ aw

R _ _ ndeer

Help Rory the Reindeer rewrite these sentences with the correct punctuation marks.

where is the dogs kennel

____

jills dog is barking

____

Wow I like your goldfish.

____

I saw elephants giraffes zebras and bears at the zoo

____

____

oh I love this book about different forests

____

____

Read the paragraph below and answer the questions on the next page.

The jungle stretches over vast expanses. For miles and miles, all you see is a stretch of land. Wait! A quick streak seems to be moving through this wide, empty space. If you look closely, you can see a spotted blur running at an unbelievable speed. It is the cheetah, the fastest animal on land.

Cheetahs have long, slender bodies that help them move at a quick pace. They use their tails to steer in the right direction.

These amazing animals belong to the cat family, just like lions and tigers. However, unlike their cousins, cheetahs do not let out loud, scary roars. They purr, just like your friendly little house cat!

Cheetahs hunt mostly during the day, either late in the morning or early in the evening. They chase their prey and pounce on them in a matter of seconds, gobbling up their meals instantly.

Which is the fastest animal on land?

___

Which family does the cheetah belong to?

___

What sound does a cheetah make?

___

When do cheetahs hunt?

___

How do cheetahs move in different directions while running?

___

Bobby wants to write a letter to all the animals he visited when he went to the jungle. Can you help him write the letter?

To,

____

____

From,

____

Look at the picture, read the lines below and complete the rest of the story.

Once upon a time, there lived a lazy shepherd boy. He didn't look after his sheep too well. Everyday, he took his sheep up the hill and left them alone while he napped under a tree. One day, ______________________________

____

____

____

____

____

____

____

Let's write a story about the jungle. Look at these animals and write a story about them.

Look at the pictures and say their names out loud. Then, fill in the blanks with the correct letter. What is the common sound you hear?

Now, read these words aloud.

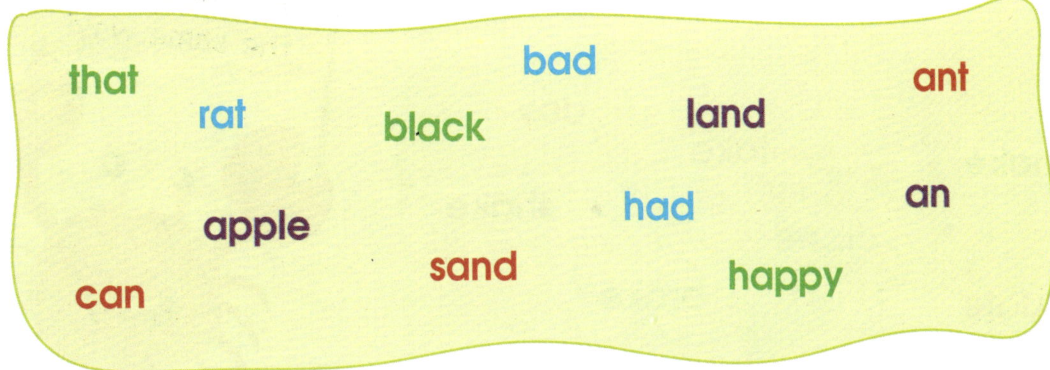

MUMBLE JUMBLE

Look at these pictures. What do you call them? Unscramble the letters and write the correct words below. Then, read the words aloud.

t d e a

____ ____ ____ ____

s k e n a

____ ____ ____ ____ ____

k e r a

____ ____ ____ ____

g t a e

____ ____ ____ ____

k e l a

____ ____ ____ ____

c e a k

____ ____ ____ ____

Now, read these words aloud.

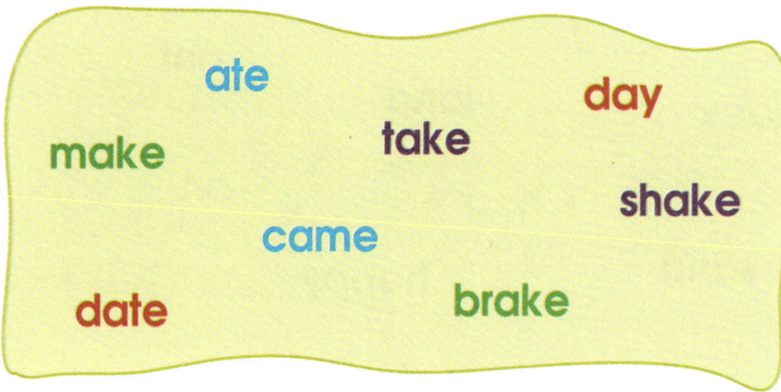

Help Ollie the Octopus complete the words on the bubbles using 'sh' or 'ch'.

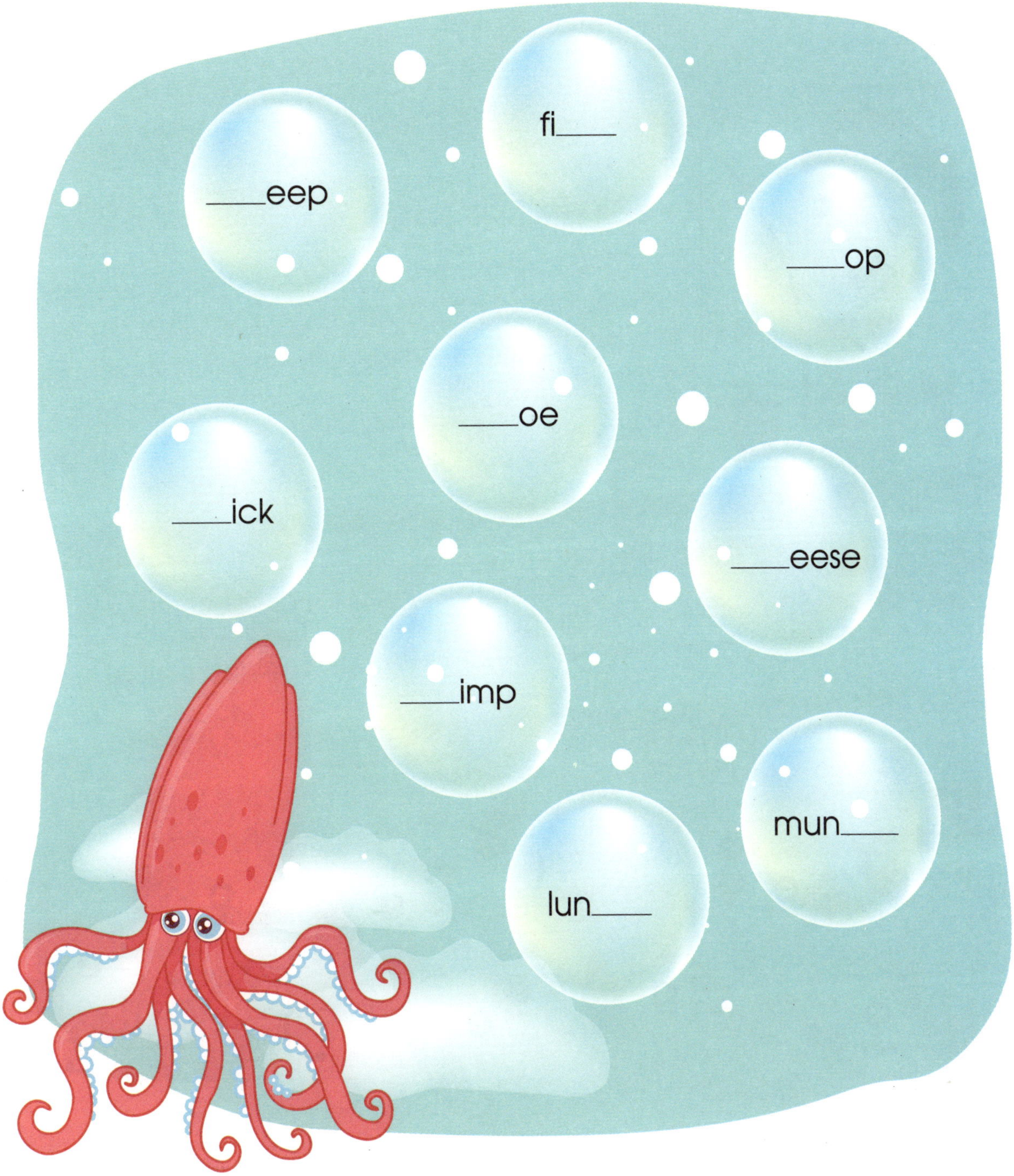

fi____

____eep

____op

____oe

____ick

____eese

____imp

mun____

lun____

PHONIC FISHING

Fish out the letters from the lake and drop them on the blanks to complete the words. You can use a letter more than once.

Help Crust the Crab fill in the crossword by naming the clues.

S

U

S H U B

S E W

I

M

S C P

H

S U G

D

THE INCOMPLETE MATCH

Help Sparkles the Starfish unscramble the 'th' words below.

t h h g r u o ____________

t e h v r i ____________

e r h t e ____________

r w o h t ____________

r s h u t h ____________

r o h e n t ____________

Help Goldie the Goldfish match the word shells to the correct bowl.

sprint
sprinkle
straw
stripe
sprig
spring
strap
string
sprout
spread

str
spr

Complete the words below using 'ee' or 'ea'.

b ______ ch	gr ______ n
l ______ f	______ l
m ______ l	b ______ k
ch ______ se	gr ______ se
fr ______ ze	br ______ ze

SEAWEED SELECTION

Choose the correct letters from the seaweeds to fill in the blanks below.

The mermaid is watching a gh______ movie.

The y______ of an egg is yellow in colour.

Dolphins are found alm______ everywhere.

F______ dances are fun to watch.

Please p______ this letter, will you?

ost

olk

OCTOWORDS

Otto the Octopus is juggling with 'oa' words, but he can't catch the right ones! Can you circle all the words with 'oa' in them?

toast
coal
foam
door
brooch
poultry
foal
toad
shoulder
cloak
floor
pour

Unscramble the letters on the submarine to form new words. Then, circle the silent letter in them.

mega

tike

panel

vedo

eack

woret

cela

tone

mile

tade

Help Sally the Seahorse hunt for words in the grid below.
Look for words that have the same letters as the shells.

c	b	t	r	a	i	n	g
l	b	b	c	d	e	f	d
a	l	n	o	w	a	y	e
y	p	m	d	a	y	h	f
q	p	r	s	i	j	i	g
m	a	y	t	t	a	i	l
y	y	z	u	v	w	x	k
a	b	p	l	a	y	c	t
d	e	l	k	l	m	n	r
f	s	a	i	l	p	o	a
p	a	i	l	q	r	s	y
g	h	n	i	s	a	y	j

ai ay

Help Frodo the Frog choose the correct word to fill in the blanks.

The rabbit's ________ is furry. (hare/hair)

Here are a ________ of turtles. (pare/pair)

Help the octopus up these ________. (stairs/stares)

The little jellyfish seems hurt and in ________. (pane/pain)

They call her a ________ fish. (plane/plain)

The lion's ________ is beautiful. (mane/main)

Help Wally the Whale add 'e' and change the words on the bubbles. Say the new words out loud; you'll notice how they sound different from the original word!

cub ________

tap ________

rip ________

ban ________

din ________

win ________

tub ________

Help Myrtle the Mermaid match the words to the correct pictures. Don't forget to say the words out loud!

book

hoof

cook

glue

room

prunes

broom

blue

RIDDLE ME THIS

Sharky the Shark has some riddles for you. Solve them and read out your answers to him.

I ring in temples, I ring in churches,
I ring in your home and in palaces.
I am a ________.

My sides are round, I'm underground,
And within me, water can be found.
I am a ________.

Supporting buildings, standing tall,
I'm made of bricks; I rhyme with fall.
I am a ________.

Hit me with a bat, or bounce me around,
I'm colourful and oh so round.
I am a ________.

Help Ollie the Oyster match the rhyming words.

fish	belly
smile	myrtle
hill	jar
dress	mile
jelly	mess
star	bill
turtle	potter
otter	dish

Smiley the Seal wants to use words with a silent 'l'. Can you help him fill in the blanks with the appropriate words?

You __________ even take a cart.

You __________ not tell lies.

I __________ help him myself if I were there.

__________ you look after my fish please?

__________ you please sit down!

We __________ preserve marine life.

could

would

should

DOBBY'S DILEMMA

Help Dobby the Dolphin fill in the blanks with words from the bubbles. Then, read them out.

I ________ I will learn to swim.

________ was a nice cake.

________ is a nice lake.

What's that roaring noise in the sky? It's ________.

The river ________ flows through London city.

________ Ganges is a sacred river in India.

________ you! I appreciate your kindness.

Trains were not working. ________ we took the bus.

the this that think

thunder therefore thames thank

STARRY SORTER

Starry the Starfish needs to sort his word bubbles. Say the words out loud and match them to the basket whose name rhymes with them.

Chloe the Clownfish is very confused between the letters 'c' and 'k'. Can you help her fill the correct letter in the blank?

______obra	______loud
______oast	______ar

zin______	pin______	______ettle
______olt	broo______	______oo______

Help Toto the Turtle fill in the blanks with words from the shell.

My mother made great __________.

The swordfish seems as if it has a __________ on it.

These animals look like __________.

Never keep animals in __________.

That __________ you see is the light of the fish.

Please be careful on the __________.

A small fish is just a __________ in the sea.

flicker

ducks

deck

shackles

speck

pickle

hammock

Read the rhyme and circle the rhyming words. Say them out loud.

Under the deep blue sparkling sea,
Lives a fish as greedy as can be.

On rotting seaweed he loves to crunch,
Apart from the same old fishy munch.

He eats floating tyres and rotting planks, too,
He once ate a monkey who escaped from the zoo.

He once ate a whole school of clown fish,
Because he thought they were a tasty dish.

He ate so much and grew so fat,
That he burst into pieces with a big,
loud SPLAT!

Use the letters given on the fish to make your own words in the bubbles. Try to make some rhyming words and connect them to each other.

P a d s g o u k m z t e l a

Connect the words to the correct boat.

I

Y

cycle
lion
ink
ivory
icy
inch
lady
India
why
eye
baby
cozy

Complete the story by filling the blanks with words from the jellyfish.

glow

allowed

window

wow

now

tomorrow

fellow

eyebrows

sailed

We went for a cruise in a ship one night. As we __________, there was a __________ in the dark. We inched our way towards it, with raised __________. The __________ by my side said, "Let's come back __________."

"__________ don't panic," I said, "sit by the __________." I __________ myself to be strong. And lo! What a sight! "__________!" A coral in the dark, is what we discovered!

TROUBLESOME TROUT

Terry the Trout jumbled up his words. Can you unscramble the letters to form the correct words? Don't forget to read them out loud!

Help Clara the Crab correct the spellings of the words below.

eest	
weast	
noth	
sourth	
baloon	
buter	
pleese	
impotant	
surprise	
groop	

Help Sharpie the Shark build his word ladder. Change one letter in each word to form a new word.

Cart	Peel	Hurt	Pine	Rose

MY FAVOURITE HOBBY

Hobbies help us develop our interests. Write about your hobbies.

Mention what interests you the most. Explain why you like it so much.

Computers have made our lives so easy! Tell us how your computer helps you.

You might want to use the internet and find out the different tasks that a computer can perform. Start your essay by listing the things it can do, then explain how it helps you.

It's holiday time and you're staying at your grandparents' house with all your cousins. Write a letter to your mother, telling her about the wonderful time you're having there.

Write about the places you visit, the games you play and the yummy food you eat.

Dear Mummy,

____

____

____

____

____

____

____

____

____

____

____

Love, ____________________________

HEALTHY MEALS

Healthy food makes us strong and helps us fight diseases. Let us create a poster to promote healthy food.

Your poster should begin with a strong message.

Theme

Write your message here.

Draw a picture.

Write the benefits of healthy food here.

ONCE UPON A DINOSAUR...

Imagine if dinosaurs were still walking on our planet today! Write a story about the time you met a dinosaur.

Did you know that you can write a story in the present tense too? Just use one tense throughout the story though!

Do you have a special box or a hiding place to keep your money? Write an essay about it.

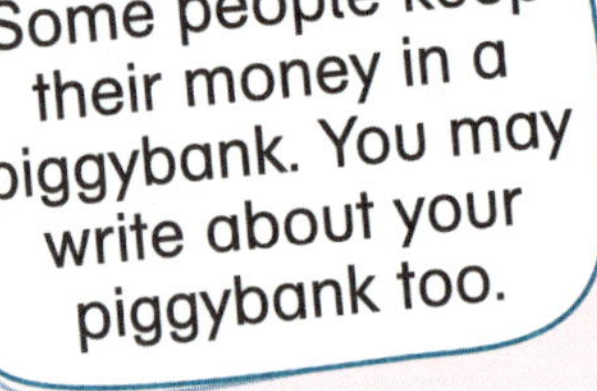

An orchard is a garden full of fruits. Write an informative essay about it.

An informative essay gives you "information" about the subject. Write about looking after plants in an orchard, gathering fruits and keeping orchards clean.

FISHY FRIEND

Imagine that you went to a beach and met a fish. It began to tell you all about its adventures in the sea. Write a story about it.

Write about how you met the fish before you dive into the story. Add a splash of adventure to it!

Imagine that you're taking the train to a faraway town. Write a diary entry about it.

A diary entry is always written in first person. Write about your journey, the people you saw, the sights you passed by, the food you ate, etc.

If clouds could talk, wouldn't they have an out-of-the-world story for us! Imagine that you're a cloud and tell us a story.

Clouds travel across the world. So you could write an adventure story.

Water is precious and not available to everyone easily. It should not be wasted. Create a poster telling everyone to save water.

Begin with a simple headline. Write facts on water shortage. End with a message that urges people to use water carefully.

Write a short headline here.

Draw a picture here.

Add your facts here.

Write your ending message.

It is important to begin the day with a hearty, healthy breakfast. Write about your favourite breakfast.

Begin by writing when you eat breakfast. Describe the different foods you eat for breakfast, then write about your favourites.

The desert is home to different animals. Look at their pictures and write a descriptive paragraph on each one.

Rattlesnake

Fox

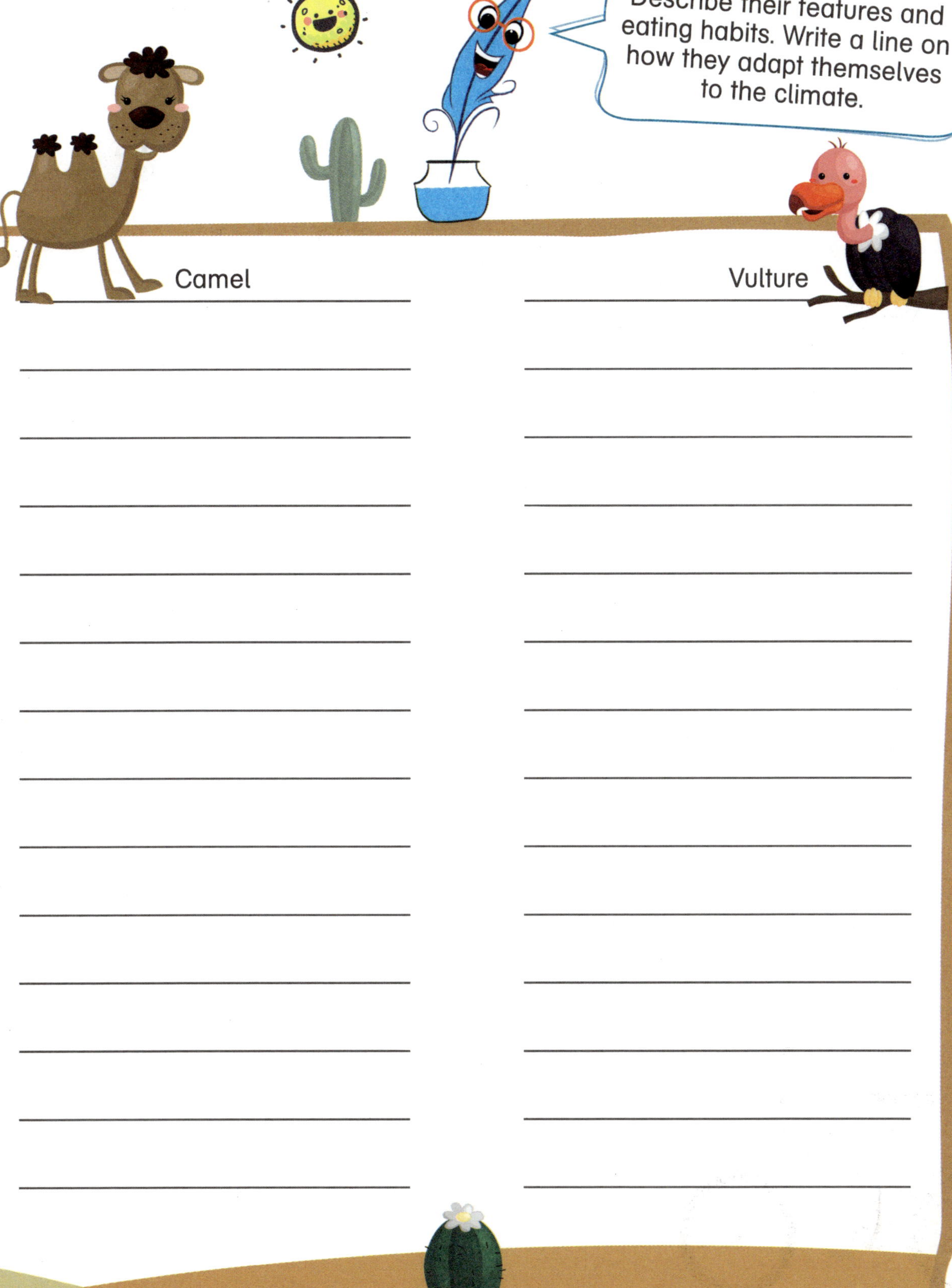
Describe their features and eating habits. Write a line on how they adapt themselves to the climate.
Camel
Vulture

Your parents gave you a new bicycle for your birthday. Write a story about it.

Describe the bicycle. Write about your first adventure on it.

What were you like when you were just a wee baby? Ask your parents and write an essay about it.

Ask your parents about the things you liked and disliked, any funny incidents you had and your favourites at the time.

You must have read stories about princes and princesses, dragons and magical creatures. It's time to create your own fairy tale!

Your story can have a main character, an evil character and a magical creature. Try and give it a happy ending.

Have you ever been to the market to buy groceries with your parents? If not, imagine that you have and write an essay about your trip.

We can buy a variety of things at the market. Write about the different shops you visited, the things you bought and the things you wanted to buy.

When you look out of the window, what do you see? Write an essay about it.

Describe the time of the day. Write about the buildings, the people you see and the things they do.

It's your best friend's birthday. Write a story on the surprise party you had for him/her.

Explain how you surprised your friend, the gifts you gave, the games you played and the food you ate. End by describing how your friend felt about the surprise.

FLY LIKE A BUTTERFLY

Imagine that you are a butterfly.
Write an essay about your life.

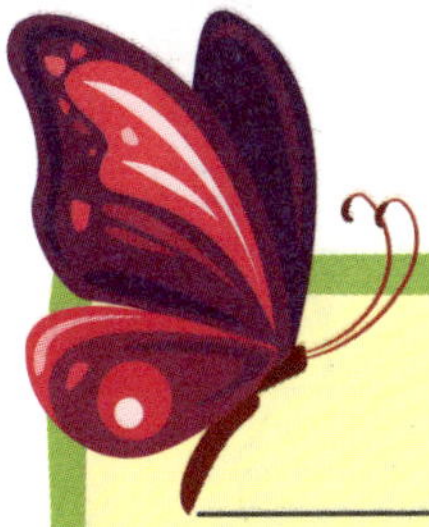

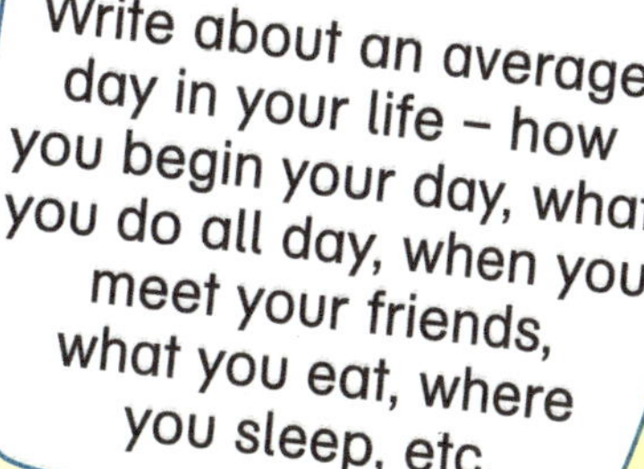

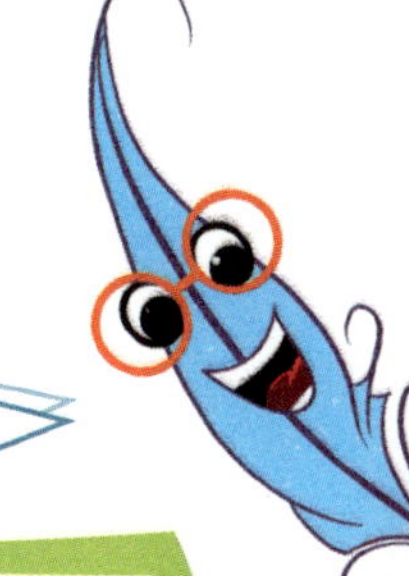

It is important to keep your body clean. Create a poster that tells everyone to stay clean.

Begin with a one-line message. Add 4-5 points on how one can stay clean – bathing, brushing, cutting nails, etc. End by asking the reader to stay clean every day.

Write your one-line message here.

____

____

Add the different ways to stay clean

____

____

____

Write your ending message.

____

Have you been to an aquarium? It has different types and sizes of fishes. Write an informative essay about it.

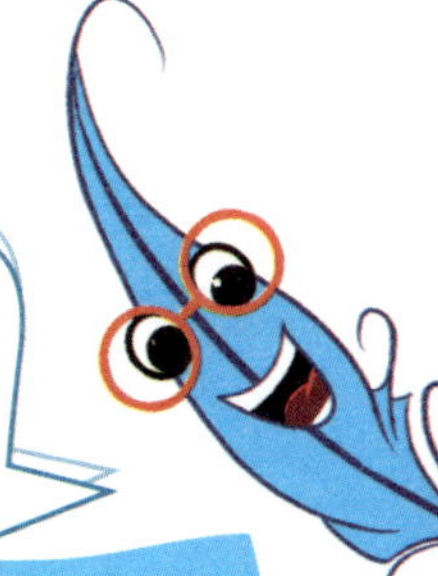

Write about the different types of sea animals found there. Explain why you would like to visit the aquarium again.

What would you do on a cold, winter day? Write different diary entries on it.

Date:

Date:

Date:

Date:

Date:

Date:

Your birthday is just around the corner and you're having a party. Write a letter to invite your cousin for the party.

Dear

____

____

____

____

____

____

____

____

____

____

Love,

____

Mention the date, describe the party and don't forget to invite your cousin's family!

Do you have a pet? If not, imagine that you have one. Write an essay about it.

Pets are like best friends. Describe your pet and talk about the things you do together. End by explaining why you love your pet.

Quilliam has some rhyming words for you. Use them to create a poem!

Your words are: tree-free, flower-shower, round-found, boy-toy, mountain-fountain, sway-play, sky-fly, run-fun.

Help the aliens reach their spaceship. Fill up the empty clouds with the missing numbers.

101									191
	112								
						163			
105			135						
								186	
	117								
					158				
110		130			160			190	200

Enter

Help the little aliens write the names of the shapes that they found on our planet.

Help Casper the Comet write the number names next to the numbers.

Number	Number name
101	
115	
120	
129	
133	
141	
148	
150	

Count the objects and fill in the blanks correctly to help Argus the Astronaut learn about space.

I can see ________ space shuttles.

I can see ________ planets.

I can see ________ comets.

I can see ________ spaceships.

Drogo the Alien is trying to find the strongest asteroid of them all. Solve the sums on the asteroid and circle the one with the highest value to help him.

13 + 30 = ______

57 + 22 = ______

62 + 34 = ______

74 + 19 = ______

19 + 54 = ______

51 + 35 = ______

SHOOTING STARS

Solve the sums on the stars below.

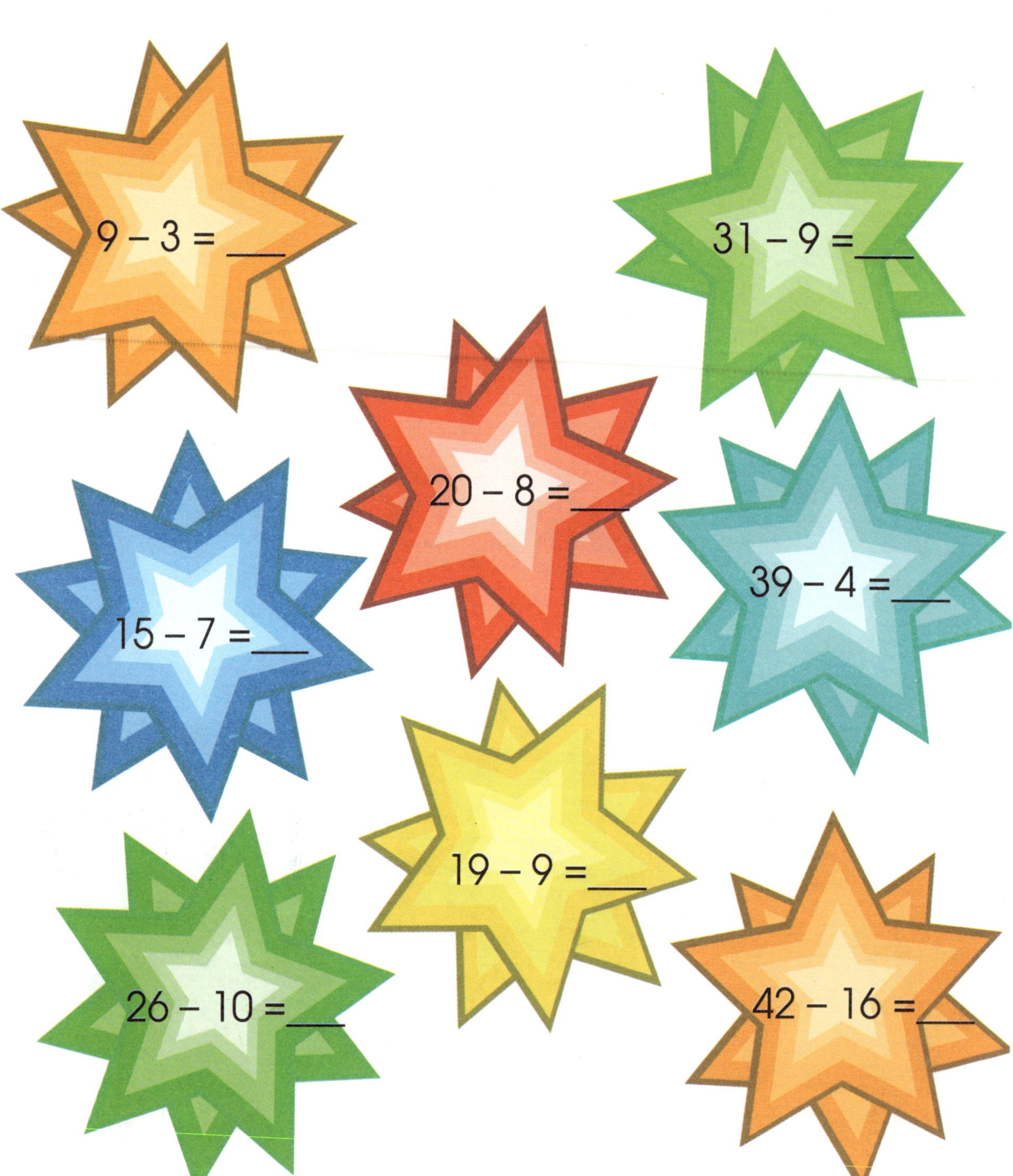

Help the aliens to skip and count their way to the spaceship!
Follow the instructions to skip and count.

Skip to the count of 2.

10,12 ☐ ☐ ☐ ☐ ☐ ☐.

Skip to the count of 10.

10 ☐ ☐ ☐ ☐ ☐ ☐ ☐ ☐ 100.

Skip to the count of 5.

20 ☐ ☐ ☐ 40 ☐ ☐ ☐.

SPACE VALUES

Andy the Astronaut wants to travel to the Math Star, but he must crack the code first. Read the place value sentences and write the correct numbers to crack the code.

Six tens and five ones = ☐

Three tens and seven ones = ☐

One ten and three ones = ☐

Nine tens and eight ones = ☐

Four tens and one one = ☐

Eight tens and two ones = ☐

Five tens and three ones = ☐

Two tens and two ones = ☐

Seven tens and four ones = ☐

Nine tens and zero ones = ☐

Zero tens and nine ones = ☐

OFF TO EARTH!

These aliens are trying to visit our planet. Read the distance on each planet and match the aliens to the correct ordinal number.

Sort the stars by connecting them to the correct basket.

15

95

86

16

23

67

42

45

32

54

Odd Numbers

Even Numbers

Help these aliens understand the values of the objects below by placing <, > or = correctly in each set.

Number the objects on the moons from shortest to longest in each row.

Circle the big spaceships and tick the small ones.

Untangle the ropes and match these sums to their values.

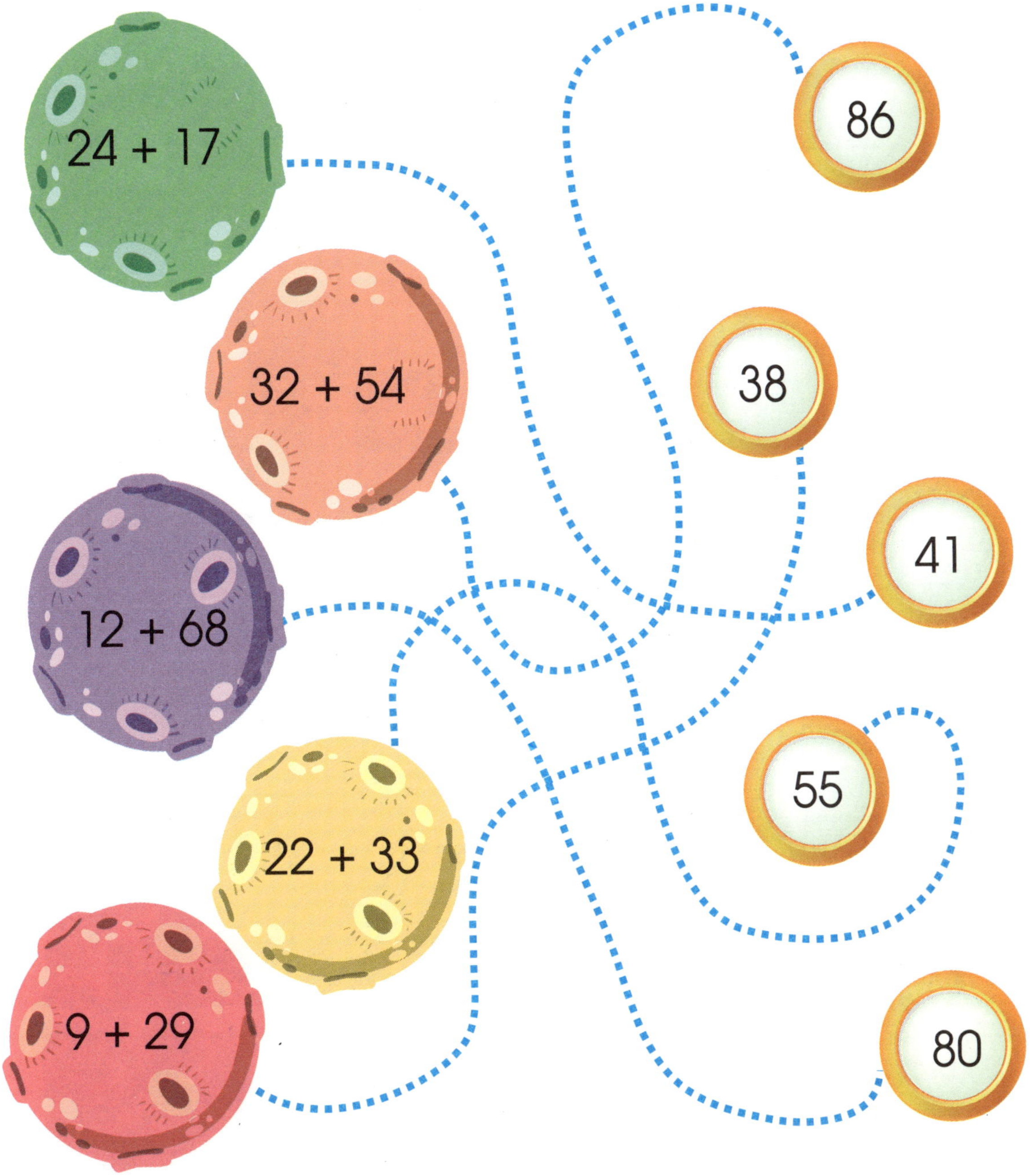

24 + 17

32 + 54

12 + 68

22 + 33

9 + 29

86

38

41

55

80

NEAR AND FAR

Number the planets according to their distance from the Sun, 1 being the nearest and 8 being the farthest.

Look at the spaceships, count the coloured ones and write their fractions alongside. One is done for you.

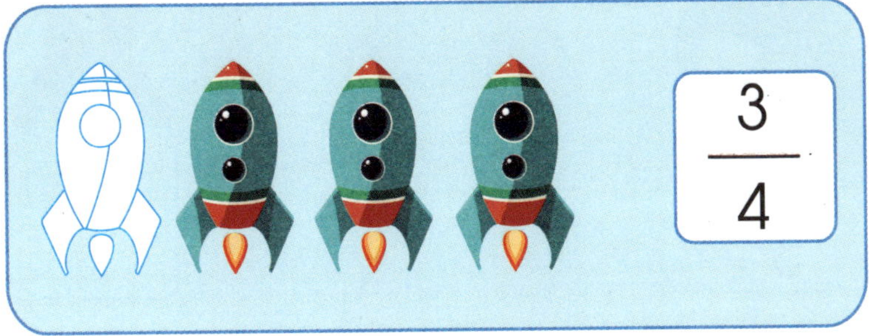

FRACTION FUN

Help these aliens learn their fractions by colouring the correct number of parts below.

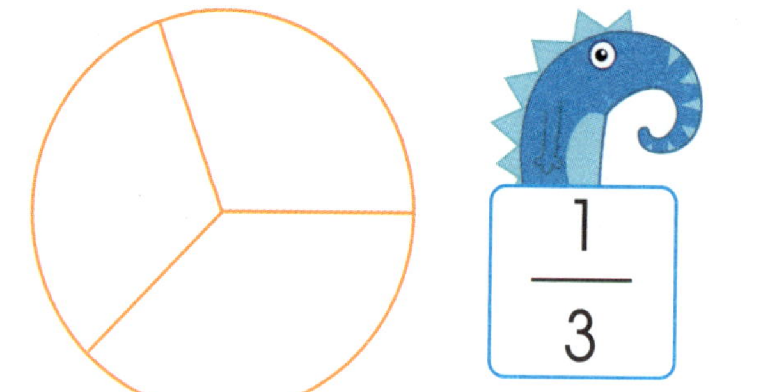

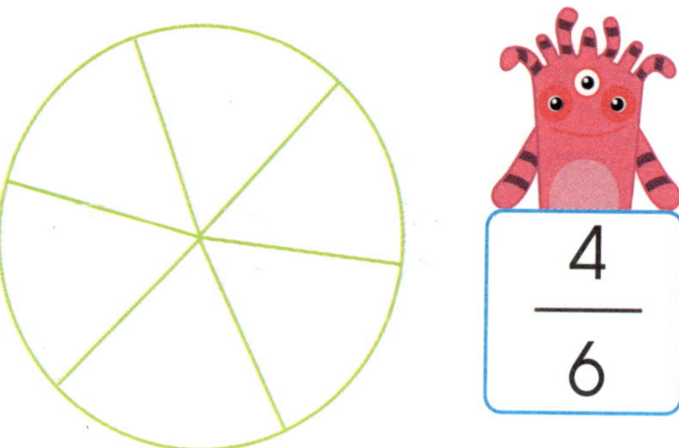

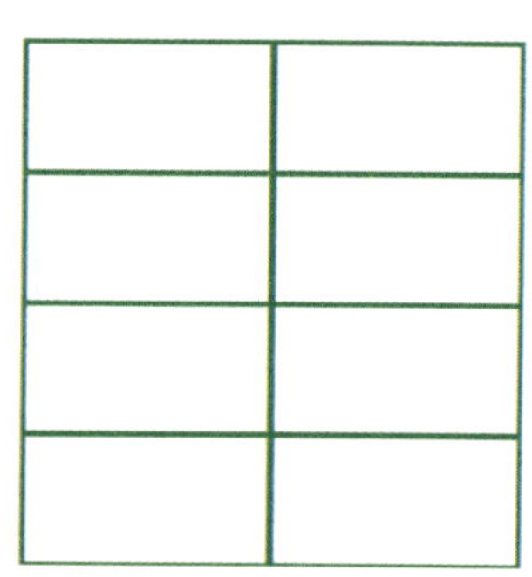

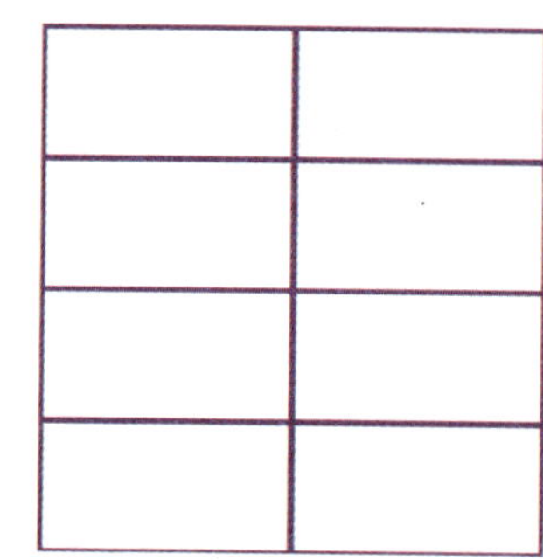

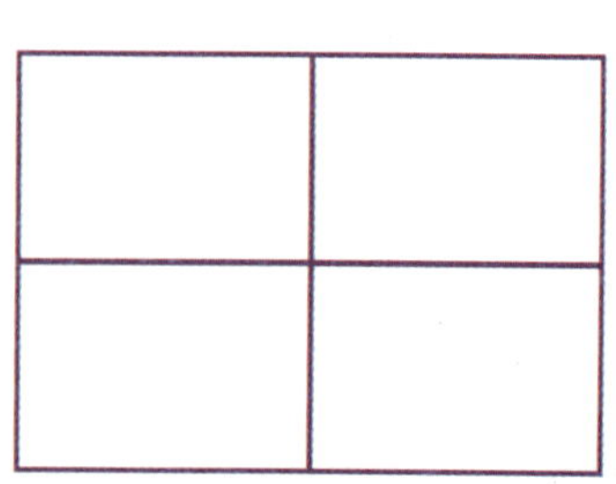

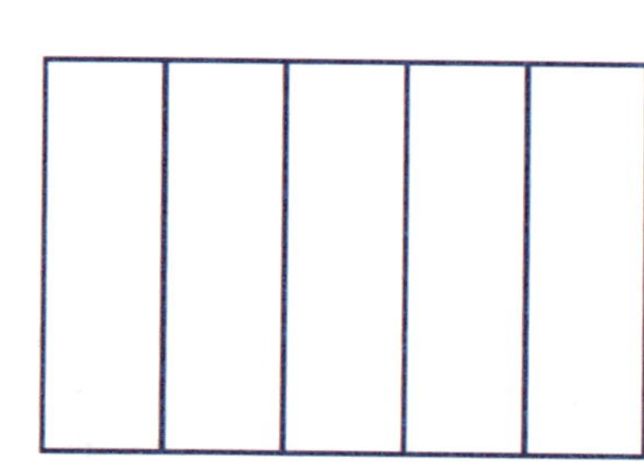

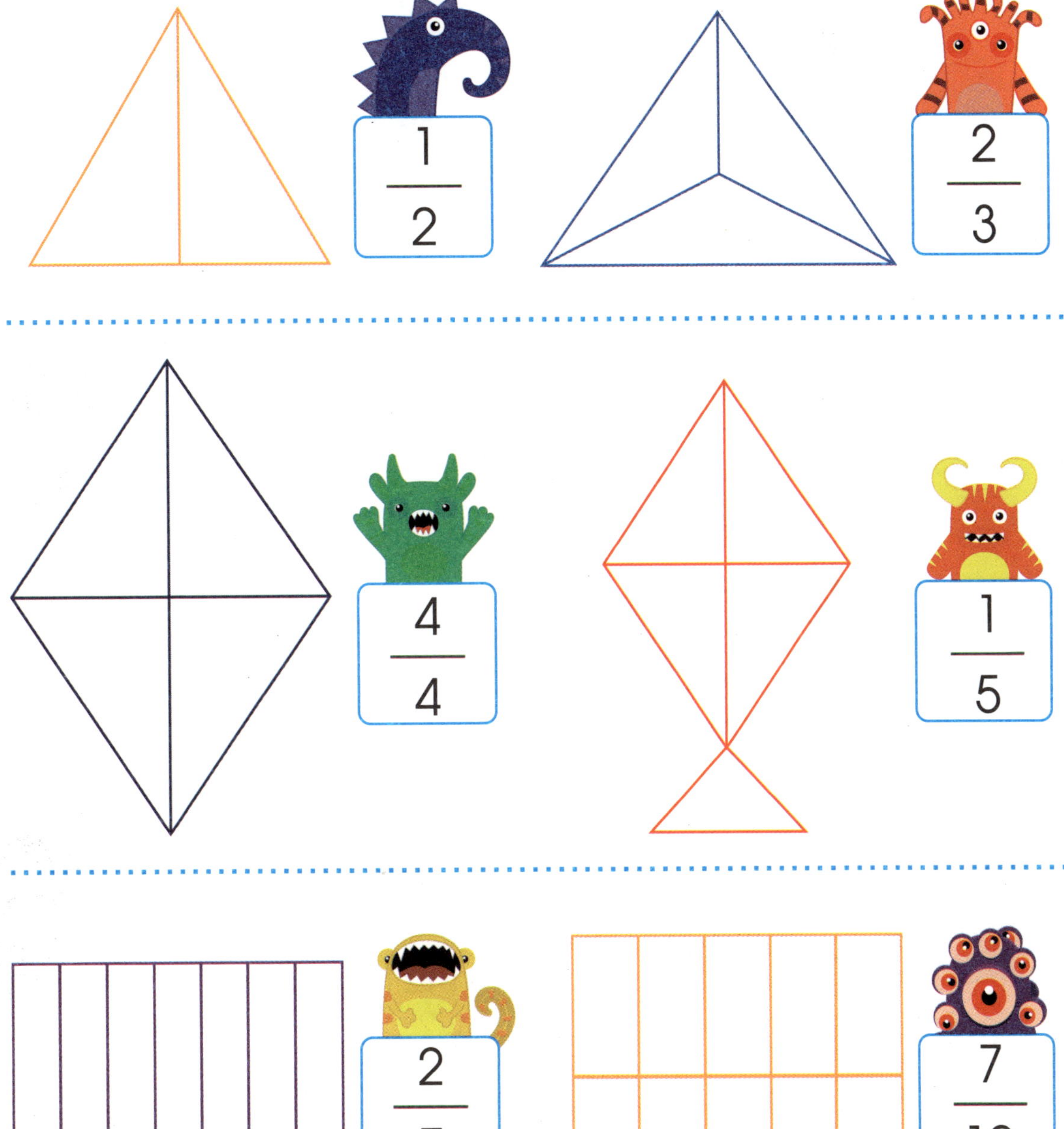
1/2
2/3
4/4
1/5
2/7
7/10

Let's solve these word problems and reach the rocket!

Angus Astroboy has 15 rockets. Aliens Bados steals 3 of them. How many does he have left?

Alien Hypo buys 16 cups of coffee. Professor Curio gives him 24 cups more. How many does he have in all?

Alien Rumbly bought 24 peaches. He distributed 17. How many does he have now?

Argo Astroboy has 10 pens. Allie Astrogirl gave him 12 more. How many does he have now?

Allie Astrogirl bought 30 spacesuits.
She gave 15 of them to her friends.
How many does she have now?

20 comets were flying in the sky.
Alien Gobbleson ate 7 of them.
How many comets are left now?

31 stars were twinkling in the sky.
A giant cloud moved and showed
14 more. How many are twinkling now?

Look at the aliens and tick the boxes under the heavier ones.

35 kg ☐	52 kg ☐
43 kg ☐	65 kg ☐
23 kg ☐	96 kg ☐
10 kg ☐	13 kg ☐

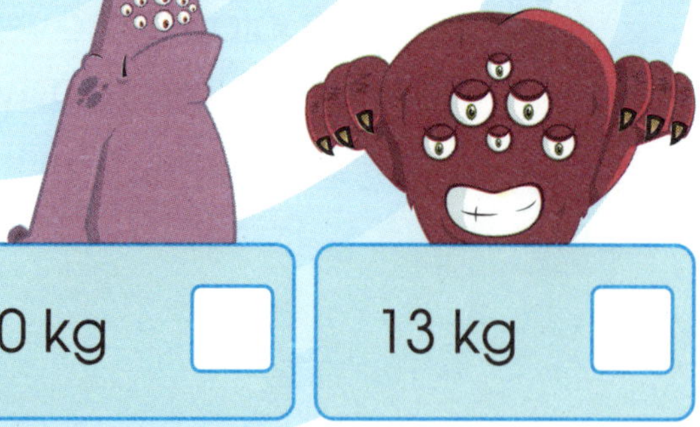

Help Addie the Alien count the notes and write their sums in the given box.

$20 + $10 = ☐

$50 + $20 = ☐

$20 + $5 = ☐

$10 + $2 = ☐

$50 + $5 = ☐

These aliens have messed up their purchase amounts!
Count the coins and solve the sums to help them out.

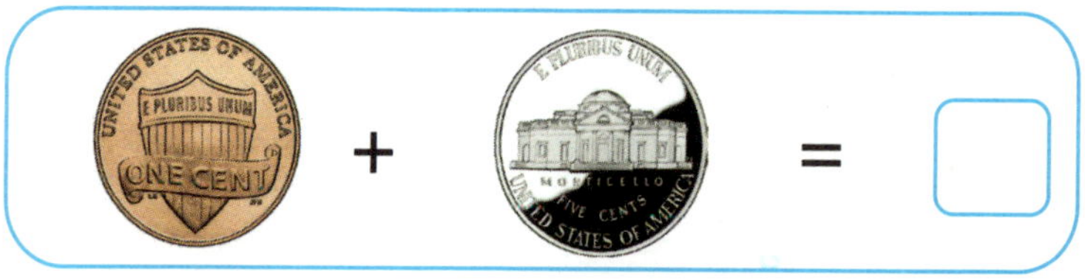

\+ = ☐

\+ + = ☐

\+ = ☐

\+ = ☐

Expand the numbers on the galaxies below.
One is done for you.

110 = 100 + 10 + 0

95 =

115 =

78 =

58 =

135 =

120 =

Look at the star rows and circle the stars with the biggest number.

123 321 245 391 156

210 152 201 125 159

66 183 445 452 354

392 376 245 352 387

These aliens bought some watches but don't know how to tell time. Can you read their watches and tell the time in them?

MULTI-TRAVELS

Help Argo the Astronaut travel to the right space station by following the path with multiples of 3.

space station

12

6

3

9

15

21

space station

18

24

27

30

space station

Solve the sums on the stars below.

6 x 3 = ____

5 x 3 = ____

12 + 4 = ____

4 ÷ 2 = ____

32 – 14 = ____

29 + 20 = ____

16 – 10 = ____

9 ÷ 3 = ____

COLOURFUL KITES

Follow the code to colour the kites below.

12 21 19 28

9 6

5 18 22

15 14

8 24

2 17

26 16

29

1

1 to 10 11 to 20 21 to 30

SPELL-O-COUNT

This Mathesaur is learning number names. Can you spell out the names of these numbers for him?

23 Twenty-three

72

83

11

66

59

94

45

Can you arrange the numbers for the Mathesaur? Write them on the leaves in an ascending order. Write them on the stones in a descending order.

Log	25 22 29 26 27				
Leaves	22	25	26	27	29
Stones	29	27	26	25	22

Log	33 31 32 34 35				
Leaves					
Stones					

Log	59 54 57 53 52				
Leaves					
Stones					

Log	91 99 94 97 95				
Leaves					
Stones					

DINO DOODLE

Connect the numbers in the correct order. Then, colour the picture.

SHAPELY MATCH

Match the shape from column "A" to its name in column "B" for this Mathesaur.

A	B
(cuboid shape)	cone
(cube shape)	cylinder
(cone shape)	sphere
(cylinder shape)	pentagon
(sphere shape)	cube
(pentagon shape)	cuboid

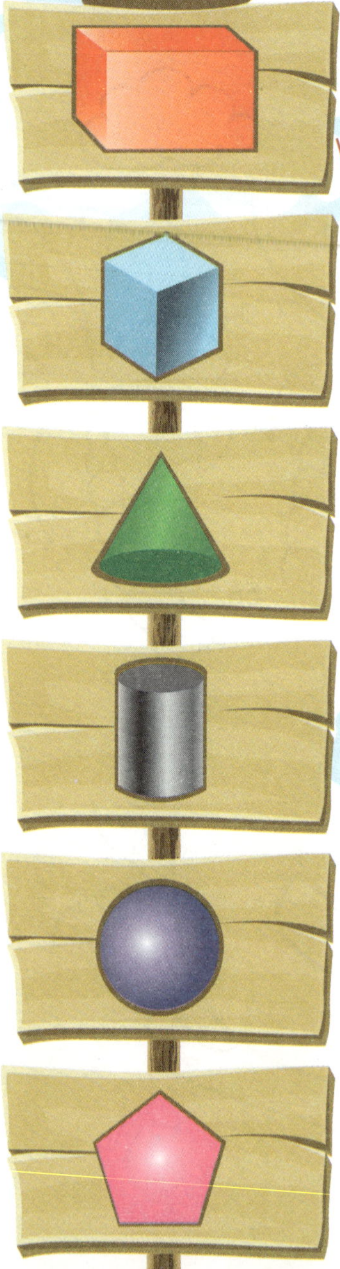

Help the Mathesaur colour the 2D shapes red and 3D shapes blue.

3D TO 2D

Help the Mathesaur match the 3D shapes to their 2D lookalikes.

Help the Mathesaur write the names of the shapes below.

Triangle ____________

____

____

____

____

____

ADDI-FUN

Let's solve some sums for the Mathesaur!

$$\begin{array}{r} 2 \\ +\,2 \\ \hline 4 \end{array} \qquad \begin{array}{r} 4 \\ +\,3 \\ \hline \end{array} \qquad \begin{array}{r} 5 \\ +\,7 \\ \hline \end{array}$$

$$\begin{array}{r} 12 \\ +\,3 \\ \hline \end{array} \qquad \begin{array}{r} 45 \\ +\,7 \\ \hline \end{array} \qquad \begin{array}{r} 76 \\ +\,9 \\ \hline \end{array}$$

$$\begin{array}{r} 88 \\ +\,12 \\ \hline \end{array} \qquad \begin{array}{r} 34 \\ +\,10 \\ \hline \end{array} \qquad \begin{array}{r} 65 \\ +\,45 \\ \hline \end{array}$$

$$\begin{array}{r} 11 \\ +15 \\ \hline \end{array} \qquad \begin{array}{r} 68 \\ +15 \\ \hline \end{array} \qquad \begin{array}{r} 58 \\ +34 \\ \hline \end{array}$$

MATH MAZE

Follow the path that has sums of 20 and help the Mathesaur reach her egg.

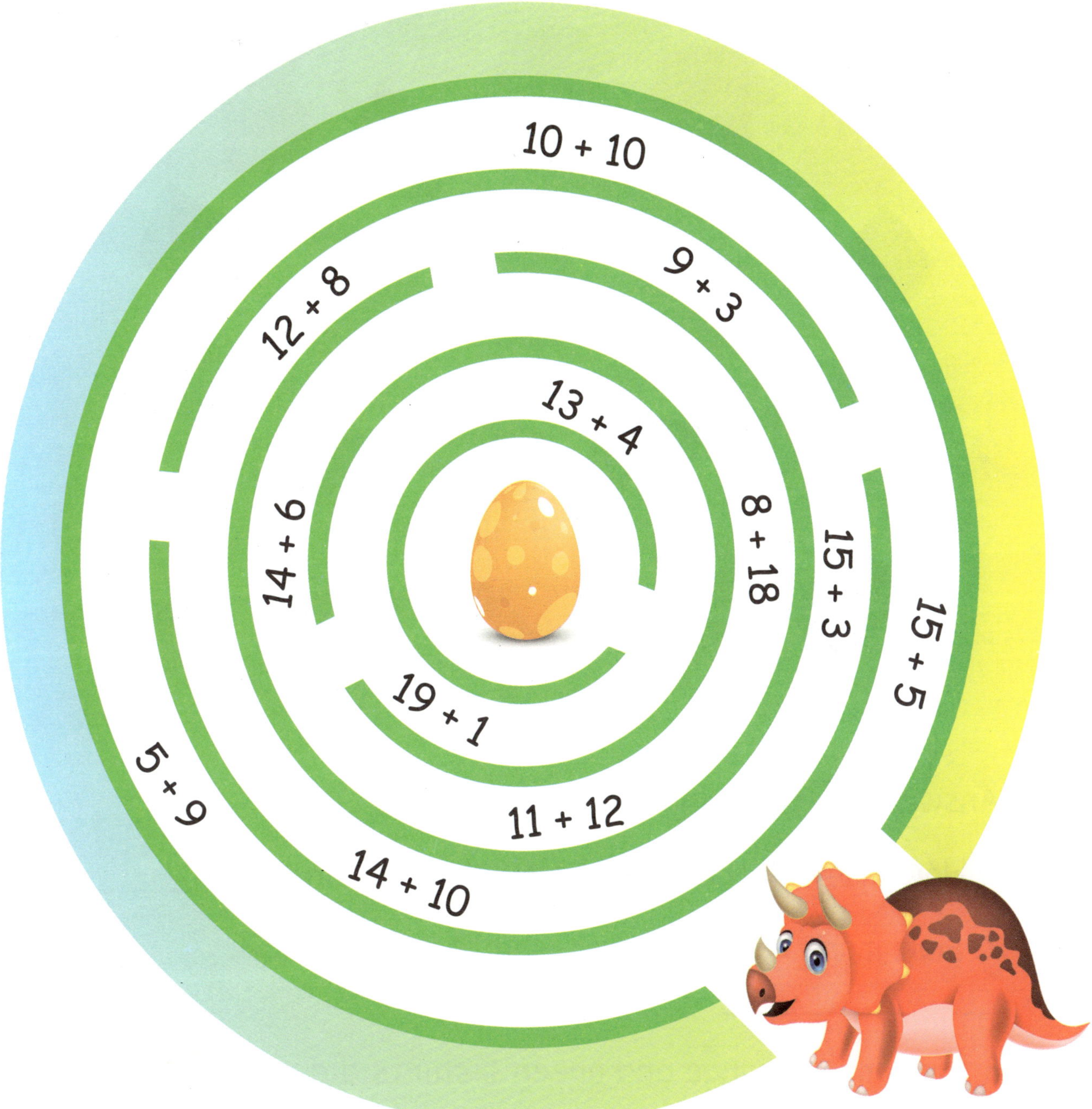

10 + 10

12 + 8

9 + 3

13 + 4

14 + 6

8 + 18

15 + 3

15 + 5

19 + 1

5 + 9

11 + 12

14 + 10

CLOTH QUIZ

Given below are the clothes that this Mathesaur found.

Answer the following:

1. How many clothes did the Mathesaur find? 20

2. How many red and pink t-shirts did he find?

____

3. How many orange and green t-shirts did he find altogether? _______________

SUBTRACTASAURS

Help the Mathesaur subtract the sums given below.

9 - 7 2	6 - 6	7 - 3
25 - 4	76 - 5	88 - 9
55 - 45	27 - 18	92 - 73

MARBLE MANIA

Subtract the marbles to solve the sums.

- = 4

- =

- =

- =

- =

This Mathesaur is starting a bakery!

Here are the cakes he has:

Here are the cakes he sold already:

Answer the following:

1. How many cakes does the bakery have in all? 17

2. How many cherry cakes does it have in all? ____

3. How many blueberry cakes does it have in all? ____

WORDY WOES

Solve these word problems for the Mathesaur.

1. Matt had 39 seashells. He gave 12 to his friend Fred and 8 to his friend Ted. How many seashells does Matt have now? ___19___

2. Ryan ate 12 bananas for breakfast, 16 apples for lunch and 22 oranges for dinner. How many fruits did he eat in all? ____________

3. Dylan had 45 marbles. He gave 18 to his sister, 12 to his brother and 5 to his mother. How many marbles are left with him? ____________

4. Mitch gave 13 flowers to his mother, 12 flowers to his aunt and 19 flowers to his grandmother. How many flowers did he give in all? ____________

5. Phil solved 23 sums yesterday and 54 sums today. How many sums did he solve in all? ____________

FUN FAIR

These Mathesaurs are buying some toys at the fun fair! Look at the money they have and match them to the toy they can buy.

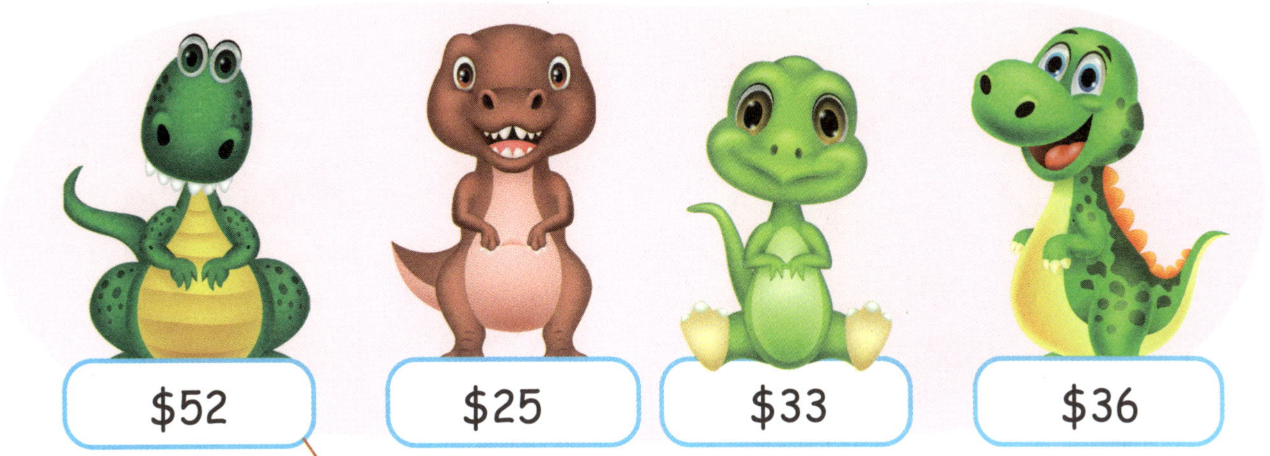

$52 | $25 | $33 | $36

$25

$36

$33

$52

BIRTHDAY GIFTS

This Mathesaur has $50 in all. How many of these things can she buy within this money? Circle the pictures, but make sure that she doesn't spend more than $50 in all!

$5

$20

$60

$15

$10

HATTABOY!

This beautiful hat is on sale for $15. Tick the notes that the Mathesaur needs to buy it.

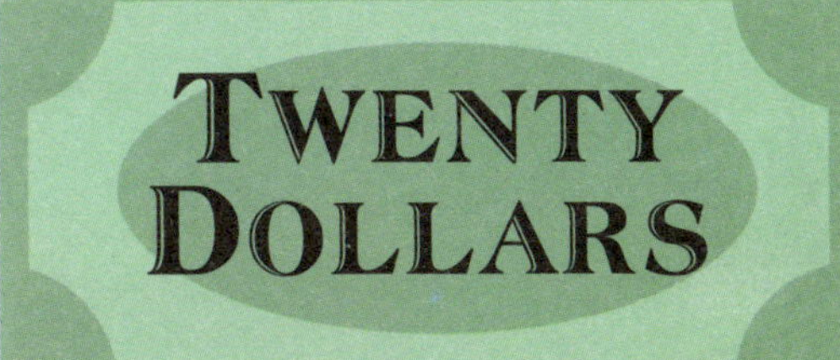

Look at the balancing machine and answer these questions for the Mathesaur.

Which fruit weighs less?

Bananas
___

Do these foods have the same weight?

___

Do these foods have the same weight?

___

Which fruit weighs more?

___

PUZZLING WEIGHTS

Solve the puzzle below.

Math Book

It takes 8 cubes to balance my book and pen together.

I know that it takes 5 cubes to balance my book by itself.

How many cubes does it take to balance my pen by itself?

____

LENGTHY TRICKS

Help the Mathesaur circle the tallest one and underline the shortest one in each set.

CLOCK-A-DOODLE-DOO

Look at the time below each clock. Draw the hands on the clocks accordingly.

5:15

6:40

4:20

8:45

7:05

3:35

TIME-TELLER

Read the time on each clock. Write the time in the empty boxes below.

Rise and shine!

7.05

Let's leave for school.

Let's go home.

Let's do homework.

Let's play!

Let's say goodnight.

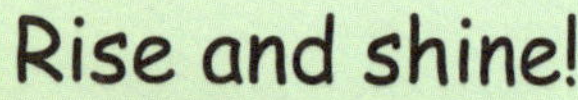

DIGI-WATCH

Look at the time shown on the digital stopwatch and help the Mathesaur to complete the sentences.

It took Amanda three hours, thirty minutes and six seconds to finish her homework.

Brown took ________________ to have breakfast.

Kelly sleeps for ________________ in the night.

Mike solves sums for ________________ every evening.

MONTHLY WOES

There are twelve months in a year.
Write their names below.

Months in a year

January	

MONTHLY MATCH

Help these Mathesaurs match the "month" leaves to the basket with the correct number of days.

HEX-A-PUZZLE

Each hexagon is made by adding the numbers in the two hexagons below it. Can you fill up the rest of the hexagons for the Mathesaur?

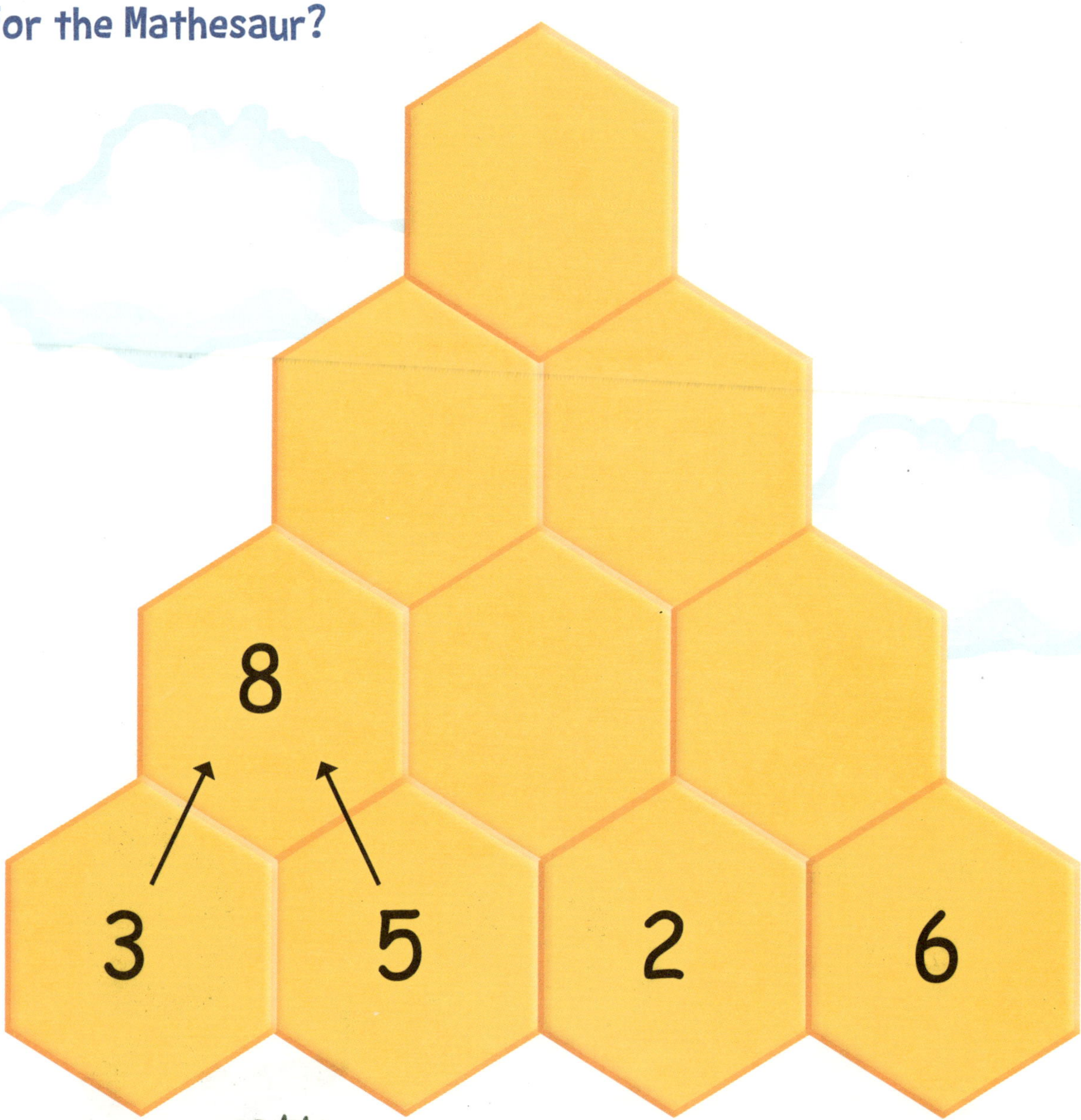

8

3 5 2 6

STICKY SOLVER

Can you remove 8 sticks from the figure below, such that the remaining sticks make 2 squares that do not touch each other. Help the Mathesaur solve the puzzle.

MATH HUNT

Help the Mathesaur by crossing out the line whose sum equals to the number written above the circle.

Make 8

4	6	5
3	2	1
3	1	2

Make 10

2	4	5
6	5	1
2	1	3

Make 12

5	1	3
2	6	4
3	2	5

Make 18

3	8	7
5	1	6
2	9	4

ADDITION

Addition is putting numbers together.

The numbers that we add are called **addends**.

The result of addition is called the **sum**.

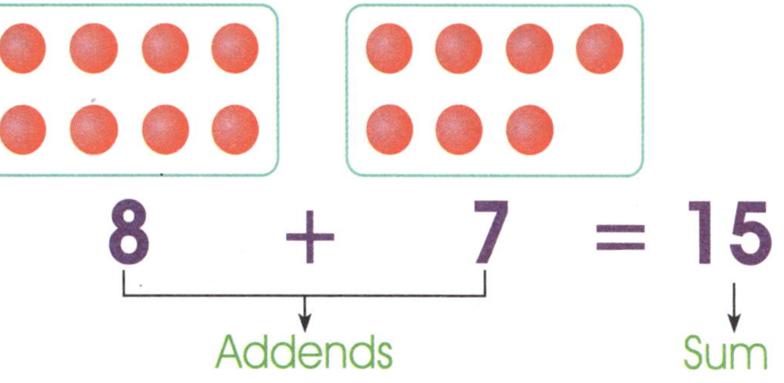

IT IS TRUE!

The sum is always greater than the numbers being added, except when one of the numbers being added is zero.

Find the sum of the following.

a. 9 + 8 = ☐

b. 7 + 5 = ☐

c. 8 + 9 + 3 = ☐

d. 5 + 8 + 7 = ☐

e. 7 + 9 = ☐

f. 8 + 4 = ☐

g. 9 + 5 + 6 = ☐

h. 4 + 3 + 5 = ☐

i. 5 + 3 + 6 = ☐

j. 2 + 5 + 9 = ☐

k. 5 + 5 = ☐

l. 6 + 7 = ☐

m. 5 + 4 + 1 = ☐

n. 8 + 1 + 1 = ☐

o. 4 + 8 + 3 = ☐

p. 5 + 4 = ☐

q. 2 + 9 + 1 = ☐

r. 3 + 6 + 2 = ☐

s. 6 + 7 + 3 = ☐

t. 9 + 1 + 7 = ☐

Challenge

Write addition sums of any 3 numbers such that they add up to 18.
How many such sums did you find?

ADDING TENS AND ONES

1. Add the **ones**

2. Add the **tens**

IT IS TRUE!
Any number +1 = next number

Add the ones. Then add the tens.

	T	O
a.	2	5
+		4

	T	O
b.	3	7
+	2	2

	T	O
c.	7	1
+	1	8

	T	O
d.	4	3
+		2

	T	O
e.	2	2
+	3	7

	T	O
f.	4	1
+	2	5

	T	O
g.	5	3
+	2	4

	T	O
h.	4	1
+	2	2

	T	O
i.	2	2
+	4	3
+	3	2

	T	O
j.	6	2
+	2	2
+	1	4

	T	O
k.	4	2
+	2	3
+	1	3

	T	O
l.	3	4
+	2	2
+	2	2

Challenge

In the addition statement below, replace the numbers at ones and tens place with other numbers such that the sum is 75.

31 + 24 ____________

ADDING TENS AND ONES WITH REGROUPING

1. Write the numbers in **expanded form.**
2. **Add** the **tens** and **ones.**
3 **Regroup** the ones.

6 tens and 10 ones + 4 ones

4. **10 ones = 1 ten,** so **carry over** 1 ten to 6 tens and **add**

= 7 tens and 4 ones = 74.

Tens	Ones		
2	8	→	2 tens and 8 ones
+ 4	6	→	4 tens and 6 ones
			6 tens and 14 ones

	①	
	2	8
+	4	6
	7	4

Write the numbers in expanded form. Then add by regrouping.

a.

T	O
2	7
+ 5	5

27= 2 tens and 7 ones

55=

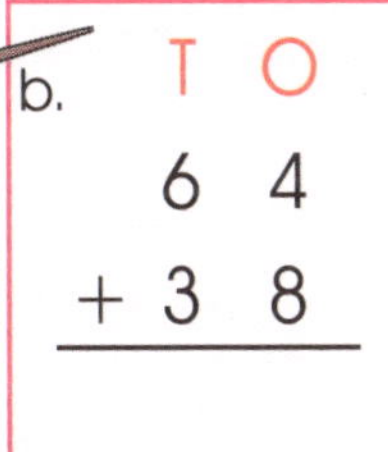

b.

T	O
6	4
+ 3	8

b.

T	O
7	2
+ 4	9

b.

T	O
1	9
+ 2	3

FAVOURITE FRUITS

Miss Lee has grown 3 types of fruits. She is making fruit salad for her nephews and nieces. They all visit her farm. This list shows the fruits the children like.

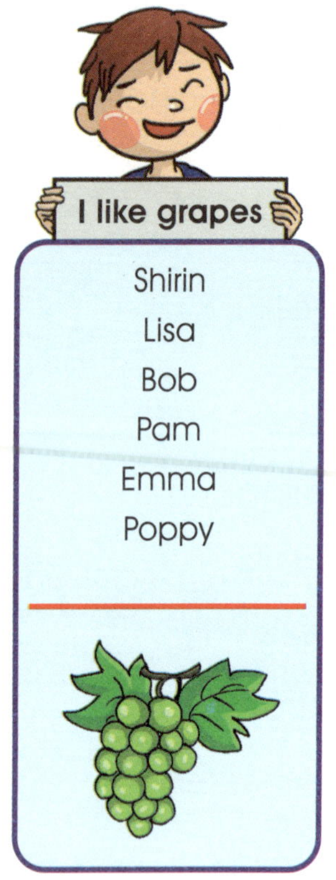

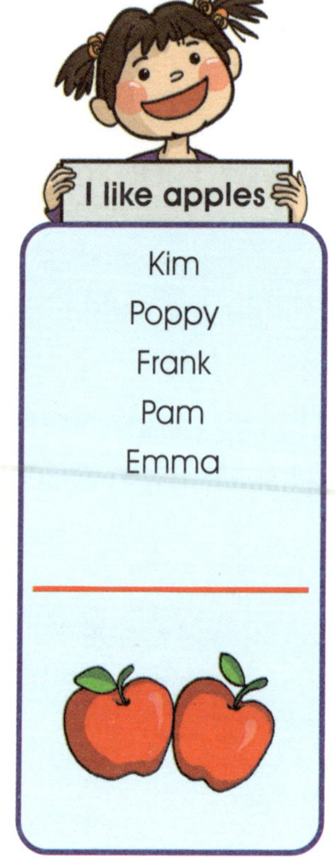

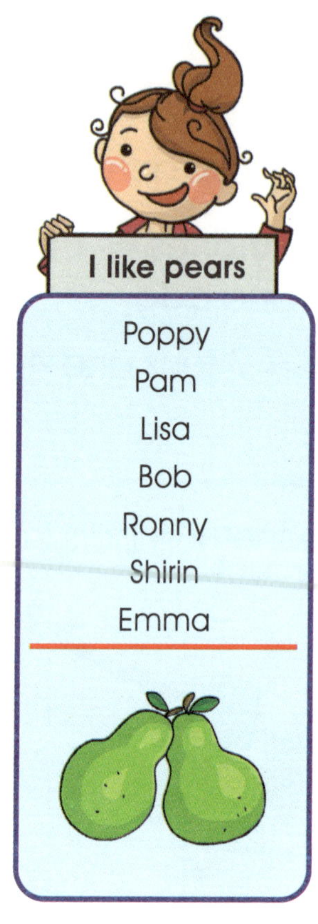

1. How many children visit Miss Lee's farm?

___

2. Name the children who like all the fruits.

___

3. Who likes both grapes and apples?

___

4. Who likes only pears?

___

5. Which two fruits should Miss Lee use for the fruit salad? Why?

___

Try this!

Which fruit do you like? Add your name to Miss Lee's list. Will this change the fruits Miss Lee would use for the fruit salad?

FAVOURITE PASTIME

Neo's friends are fond of different pastimes.

- Help him make a list of pastimes that are popular among his friends.
- Use the information from the pictures to complete the table.

Pastime	Number of Children
skating	3

Which pastime is the most popular among Neo's friends?

____

TALLY CHART

A tally chart is made using tallies to record data or information.

Susan made a tally chart to record the favourite subjects of her classmates. Help her answer the questions by interpreting the chart.

Subject	Tally count
Math	𝍸 𝍸
Reading	𝍸 𝍸 𝍸 𝍷
Science	𝍸 𝍸 𝍸 𝍸
Social Science	𝍸 𝍸 𝍷𝍷𝍷
Writing	𝍷𝍷𝍷𝍷

1. How many of Susan's classmates have Science as their favourite subject?

____

2. How many more students like Reading than Math?

____

3. Did more students choose Math or Social Science?

____

4. Which subject has the most votes?

____

5. Which subject has the least votes?

____

Try this!

Make a tally chart to show the favourite subjects of your classmates.

Where are you placed in the tally chart?

SCORE HIGH!

Five students of Grade 2 participated in the Science Quiz. They made a tally to show the marks they had scored so far.

Student	Tally count
	𝍸 𝍸 𝍸 𝍸 𝍸 𝍸 ||
Joy	𝍸 𝍸 𝍸 𝍸 |||
	𝍸 𝍸 𝍸 𝍸 𝍸 ||||
Jill	

- Something has gone wrong with the tally chart. Correct it so that it shows all the information.
- One of the students is hoping to win the quiz. Who do you think it might be?

____

- Write down 5 things you know from the tally chart. Take help of the hint box.

____

____

____

____

____

Hint Box!

Number of children participated in the quiz

Who scored the highest?

Who scored the lowest?

Scored more than Joy

Scored less than Jill

ON THE SEA SHORE!

Martha saw wonderful sea creatures when she was on a holiday. Help her make a tally chart to list the creatures.
These pictures show what she saw.

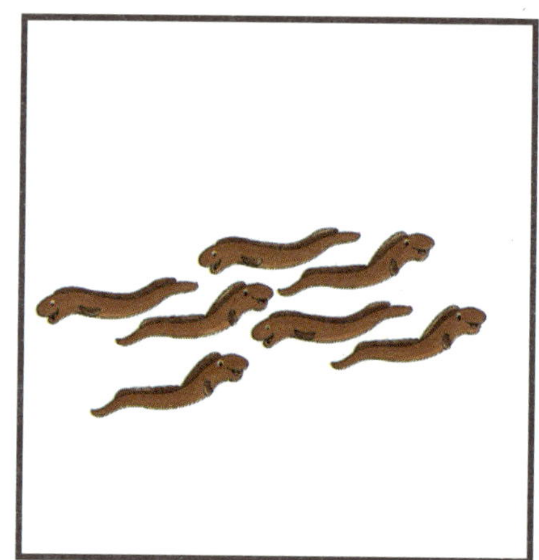

Use the information on page 188 to help Martha make a tally chart.

Sea creature	Tally count

Use the chart to answer these questions.

1. How many of each creature did Martha see?

angelfish ______________ turtle ____________ shark ______________
crab ______________ jelly fish____________ starfish ______________

2. Which creature did she see the most?

____

3. How many crabs did she see more than the turtle?

____

4. How many creatures did she see in all?

____

Try this!

Imagine you saw 2 more of each type of sea creature than Martha. How will your tally chart change? Make a new chart.

FREQUENCY TABLE

The **frequency** of a data value is the number of times the data value occurs. For example: If 3 students have a score of 55 in mathematics, then the score of 55 is said to have a frequency of 3.

A **frequency table** is constructed by arranging these collected data values.

Mr. Paul has made a frequency table to show the sales of story books last week. Read the table and answer the questionnaire.

Story Book	**Number of books sold**
Cinderella	1000
Rapunzel	1560
Snow White and the Seven Dwarfs	2380
Beauty and the Beast	1300
Pinocchio	2000
Peter Pan	1220

1. Which is the best-selling story book?

2. Which book sold fewest the last week?

3. How many copies did Mr. Paul sell of each book? Arrange them in the order of fewest to the most.

4. Which book should Mr. Paul always have in stock to get good sales?

HOLIDAY TIME

Linda is planning for a travel package. She made a tally chart to show holiday bookings by different people of her city.

Country	Tally	Frequency
Italy	卌 ||	7
Bangkok	卌 卌 卌	15
France	卌 卌 卌 ||||	19
Australia	卌 |	6
Singapore	卌 |||	8

Complete the frequency table and answer the questions.

1. Which was the most popular country to visit?

____

2. Which countries did more than 10 people book?

____

3. Which countries did less than 10 people book?

____

4. Linda needs to make arrangements for 3 more people in Bangkok, Italy and Australia. What would be the number of bookings for these countries now?

   Bangkok ______________

   Italy ______________

   Australia ______________

PICTOGRAM

A pictogram is a graph used to compare data using pictures or symbols.

Ben made a pictogram to record the number of little creatures in his garden. Check to see if he has got it right. Add more circles if they are needed and cross out any that are not needed.

= 1 creature

Ants	● ● ● ● ● ●
Caterpillars	● ● ●
Butterflies	● ● ● ●
Bees	● ● ● ● ● ●
Ladybirds	● ● ● ● ●
Beetles	● ●

How many of each creature does Ben find?

ants __________ caterpillars __________ butterflies __________

bees __________ ladybirds __________ beetles __________

Mr Roger has collected some musical instruments for the orchestra.
Look at the pictures given below.

Complete the pictogram to show the different types of instruments he has collected.

▲ = 1 instrument

Number of Instruments

guitar	trumpet	piano	drum	violin

How many of each instrument does Mr Roger have?

violin ____________ drum ____________ guitar ____________

trumpet ____________ piano ____________

Try this!

Make up five questions from this pictogram to ask your friend.

AT THE STORE

Miss Carol recorded the number of different pieces of clothing in her store. She made some notes. Complete the frequency table for her.

Piece of clothing	Frequency

1. How many of each piece of clothing does Miss Carol have?

   Trousers ____________ Shirts ____________ Skirts ________

   Dresses ____________ Shorts ____________

2. How many are only for boys? ____________ only for girls? ____________

3. How many pieces of clothing does she have altogether?

   ____

4. How did you work it out?

   ____

Try this!

What will be the total number of pieces of clothing if 5 is added to each item?

CHRISTMAS PRESENTS

The students in Kelly's school voted for the presents they wanted for Christmas. The pictogram shows what the students asked for.

 = 2 presents

Number of gifts

Remote control car	Skates	Chocolates	Board game	Water colours	Soft toy	Robot

1. How many of each present did the students vote for?

remote control car ____________ skates ____________

chocolates ____________ board game ____________

water colours ____________ dress ____________

soft toy ____________ robot ____________

SORTING OBJECTS

Bob sorted objects according to their colour. Is his pictogram correct? Correct it for him.

 = 2 objects ◗ = 1 object

Bob's List	
Red	13
Green	16
Blue	11
Yellow	20

Bob's List	
Brown	25
White	5
Black	8
Pink	12

	● ● ● ● ● ● ◗
Blue	● ● ● ●
	● ● ● ◗
Yellow	● ● ● ● ● ● ● ●
	● ● ● ● ● ● ● ● ● ● ● ●
	● ● ●
	●
Pink	● ● ● ●

Try this!

Look around your room and sort different objects according to their colour. Make a pictogram to show this.

JAM FACTORY

Henry's food store packs jam bottles every day. Use the information in the list and make a pictogram to show the data.

Monday	25
Tuesday	45
Wednesday	40
Thursday	30
Friday	50
Saturday	22
Sunday	15

Monday	Tuesday	Wednesday	Thursday	Friday	Saturday	Sunday

Try this!

How many bottles of jam were packed in the week? What is the easiest way to work it out?

BAR GRAPH

A bar graph uses bars to show a picture of the data collected.

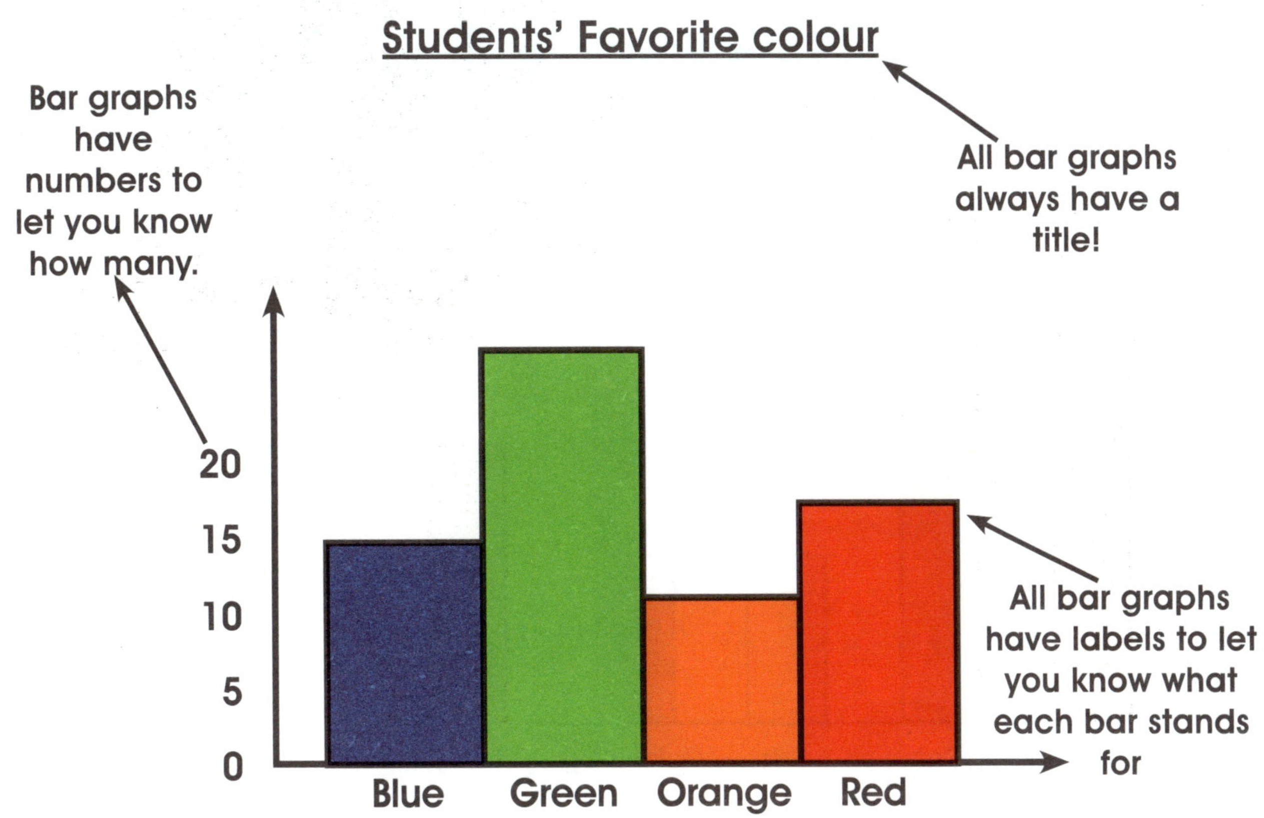

We use a bar graph to compare data.

Steps to construct a bar graph:

- Gather data
- Write a title
- Draw a horizontal line and a vertical line
- Add numbers on vertical line
- Write labels on horizontal line
- Determine the intervals
- Draw bars to show your data

PETS AT HOME

Polly and her classmates have pets. The bar chart shows how many children have these pets.

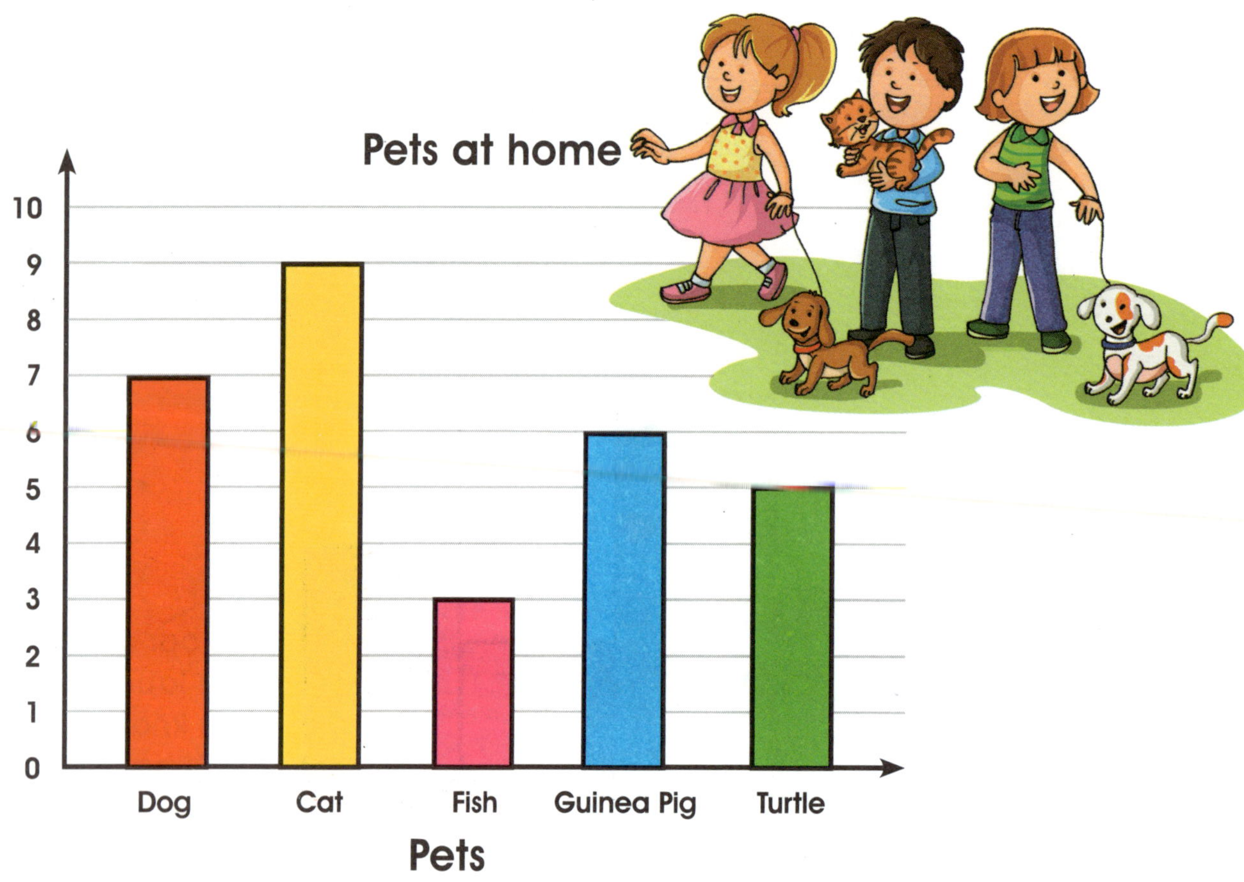

1. How many of each pet does the graph show?

dog ______________, cat _________________, fish _____________

guinea pig _________, turtle ________________

2. Which pet do most children have?

____

3. Which pet do least children have?

____

PUPPET SHOW

Kelly and friends wanted to organise a puppet show. They voted which puppet to put on the show. The bar chart shows the results of the voting.

Puppet Popularity

1. How many children voted for each puppet?

   clown ____________, pirate ______________, sailor ________________

   prince ____________, princess ____________, magician ______________

2. Which puppet should the children choose?

   ____

3. Which puppet is not popular among the children?

   ____

TEMPERATURES IN MOLLY'S TOWN

The bar chart shows the average temperature of Molly's town last year. Study the graph and answer the questions.

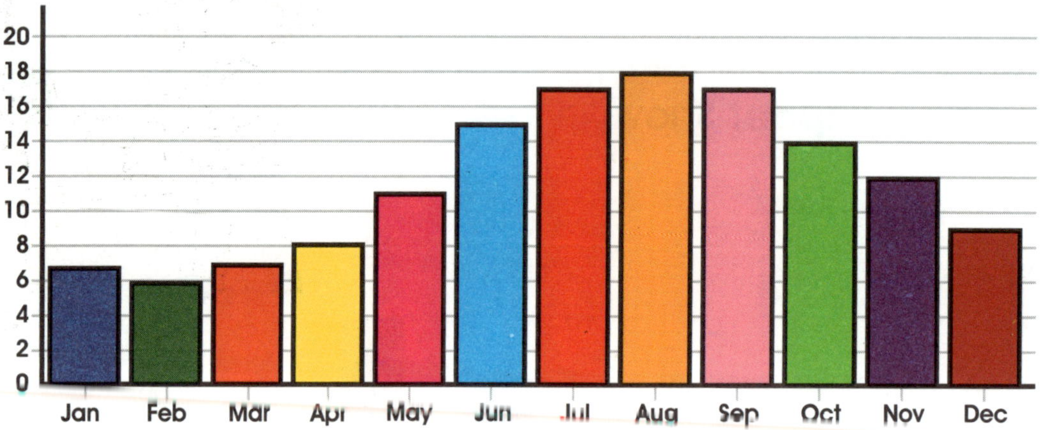

1. What is the average temperature for these months?

   January ___________, April ___________, June ___________

   August ___________, October _________, December ___________

2. Which is the hottest month?

   ____

3. Which is the coldest month?

   ____

4. What is the difference between the temperatures of August and January?

   ____

Try this!

Which is the best month to go on a beach holiday to Molly's town?

Quick tip!

The more the temperature, the hotter it is. The less the temperature, the colder it is.

CREATING A BAR CHART

Before you create a bar chart, let's brainstorm the steps you need to follow.

The frequency table shows the favourite snacks of people at Mac's restaurant.

Snacks	**Number of people**
Burger	10
French fries	8
Noodles	6
Cheese puff	12
Corn chips	15

Use the following to make a bar chart.

1. What will your title be?

____

2. What will you call the horizontal line?

____

3. What labels will you use on the horizontal line?

____

4. What will you call the vertical line?

____

5. What numbers will you use on the vertical line?

____

Now make a bar chart in your notebook.

FLOWERS IN THE GARDEN

Nora made a frequency table to show the number of flowers in her garden.

Name of flower	Frequency
Rose	15
Lily	11
Tulip	9
Sunflower	12
Daisy	8
Orchid	6

Make a bar chart to show this information.

THE SCHOOL LIBRARY

New books on different subjects have been added to the school library. Look at the picture and complete the frequency table. Then draw a bar chart on page 206 to show this data.

Subject	Number of books

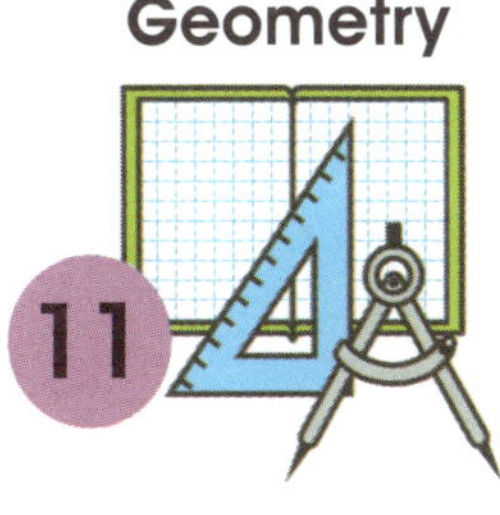

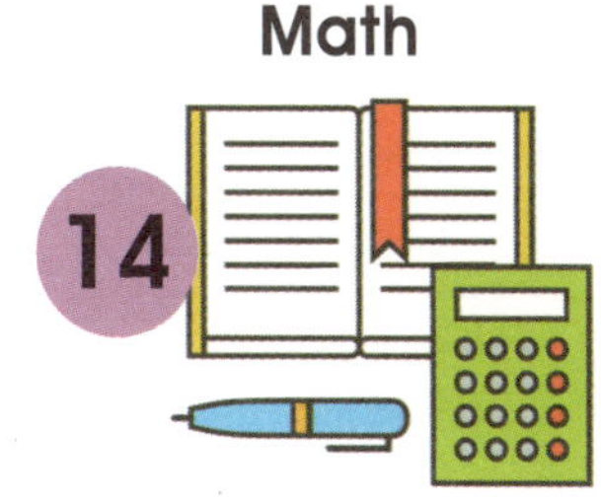

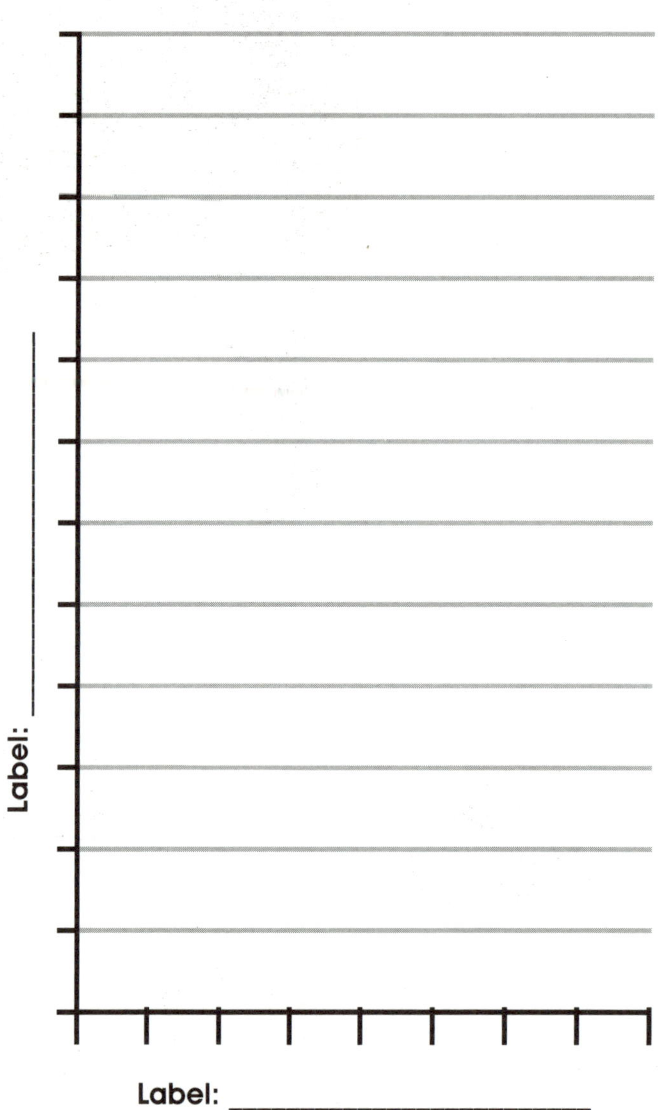

Try this!

How many new books are added to the school library altogether?

COOKIES FOR SALE

The picture below shows the number of different cookie packets ordered at Mr. Paul's bakery.

Complete the frequency table.

Cookies	Number of boxes ordered

Try this!

Make notes from the above data to make a bar chart

COOKIES FOR SALE

Use your frequency table on page 207 and make a bar chart.

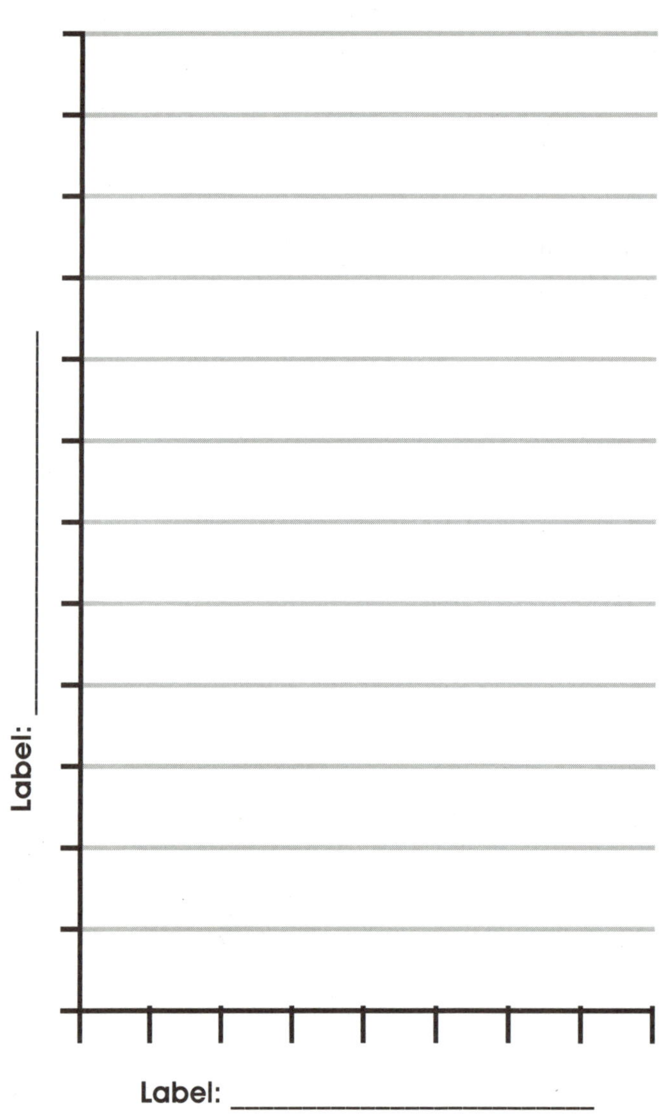

VENN DIAGRAM

A Venn diagram is a visual tool used to compare and contrast two (sometimes three) different things. A Venn diagram is made up of two large circles that intersect with each other to form a space in the middle.

Steps to make a Venn diagram

Compare- how two things are alike or similar

Contrast- how two things are different

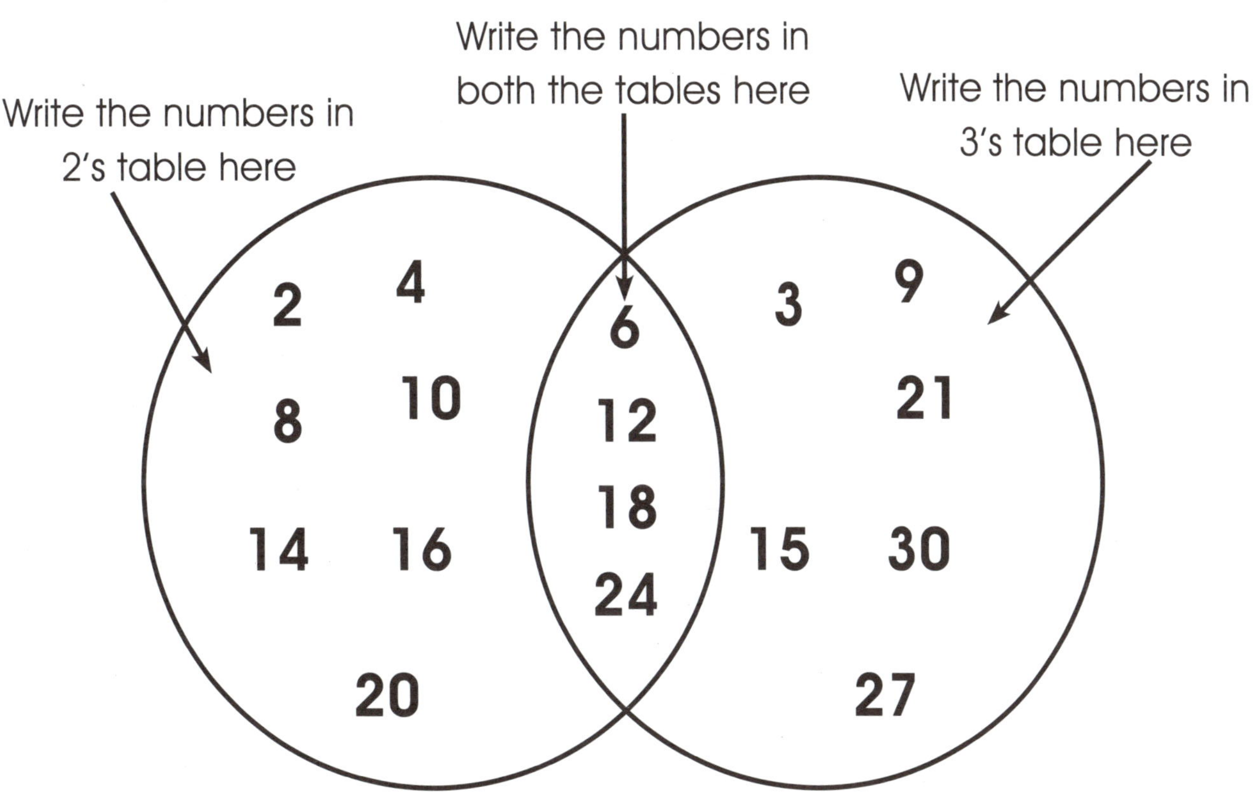

Venn diagram to compare numbers in 2's table and 3's table

Try this!

Make a Venn diagram to compare numbers in 2's table and 6's table.

STRAWBERRY OR VANILLA

Ronny asked his friends if they liked strawberry ice cream or vanilla. He recorded what they said in this Venn diagram.

1. How many of Ronny's friends like:

   Strawberry _________, Vanilla _________, both_________.

   Only strawberry _________, Only Vanilla _________

2. How many friends did Ronny ask?

Try this!

Ask your friends their choice between strawberry and vanilla. Make a Venn diagram to show your results.

AMAZING ANIMALS

James studied about many animals. Help him sort the animals that live on land and in water. Help him make a Venn diagram.

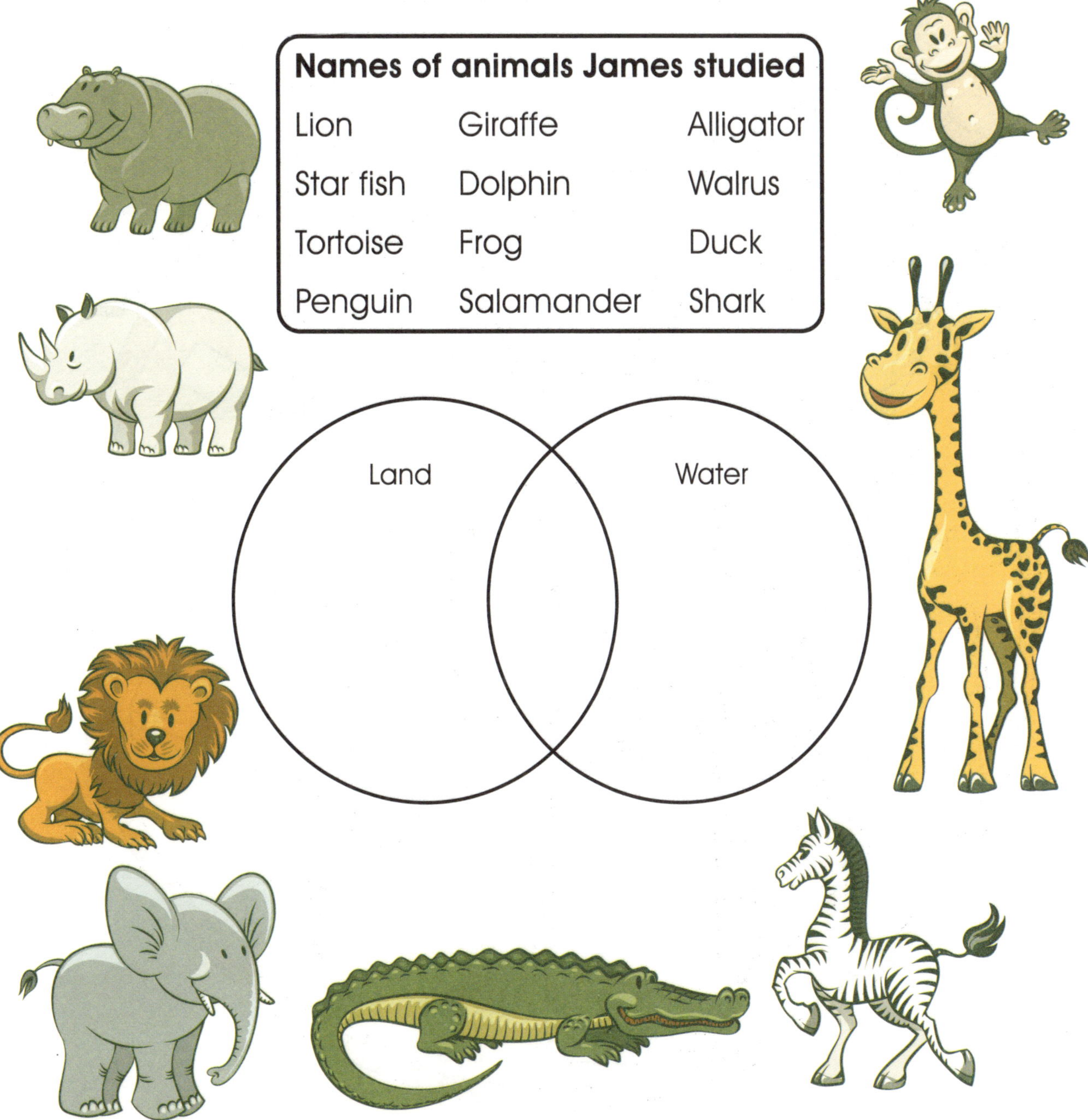

Names of animals James studied		
Lion	Giraffe	Alligator
Star fish	Dolphin	Walrus
Tortoise	Frog	Duck
Penguin	Salamander	Shark

Try this!

Think of 3 questions you can ask your friend from the Venn diagram.

IDENTIFYIN G PLANE SHAPES

Identify each shape. Then write its name matching its number in the table below.

3-	4-	5-	6-
7-	8-	9-	10-

QUADRILATERALS

A quadrilateral is a closed figure with four sides and four angles.

They can be grouped by sides, angles, length and parallel sides.

Cross out the shapes that are not quadrilaterals. Then write the correct name for each quadrilateral.

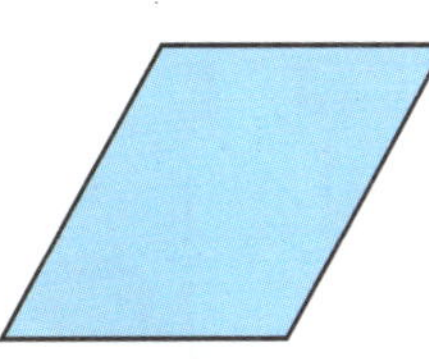

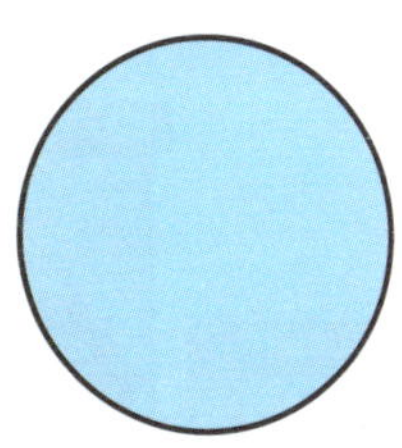

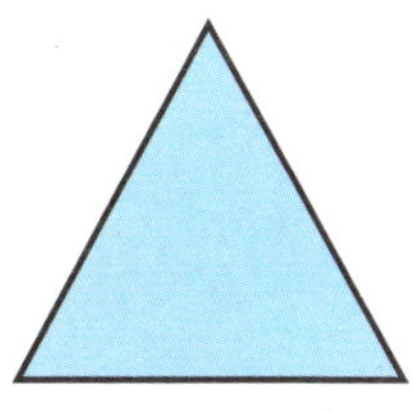

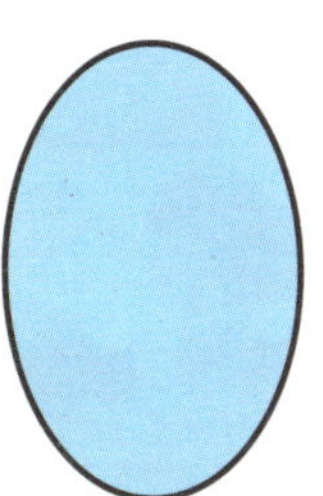

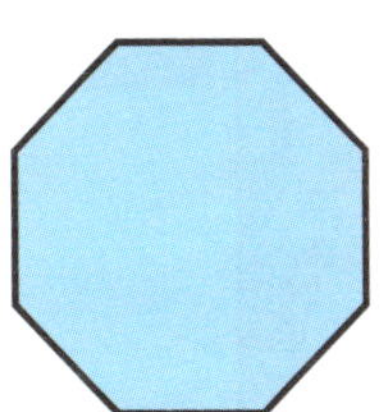

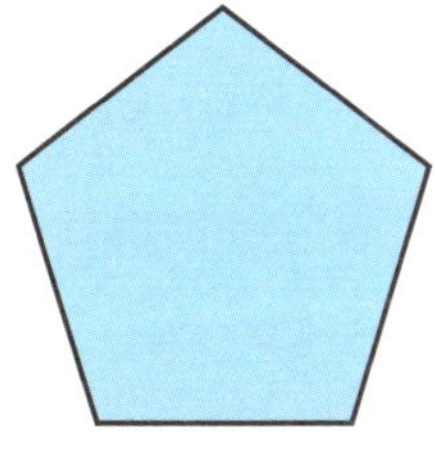

CHALLENGE

Fill in the table to compare the quadrilaterals.

Figure	Number of sides	Parallel sides	Angles
Square	4 equal sides	2 pairs of parallel sides	4 right angles

FAMILY

A family is a unit of parents and their children living together.

Look at the pictures and write what families do together.

Draw your family doing something together.

FAMILY

This is Jack's family. Use these words to label the picture.

father, mother, grandfather, grandmother, brother, sister

Write if these statements are true or false.

1. James is Jack's grandfather. ________
2. Linda is Alice's daughter. ________
3. Neo is James's father. ________
4. Jack is Doris's grandson. ________
5. Alice is James's wife. ________
6. Doris is Linda's grandmother. ________
7. James is Linda's father. ________
8. Jack is Alice's son. ________

OUR NEEDS AND WANTS

Needs are things without which it would be difficult to live or survive.

Wants are things we would like to have but don't need to live.

Draw a line from the word to the picture it goes with.

1. need
2. want

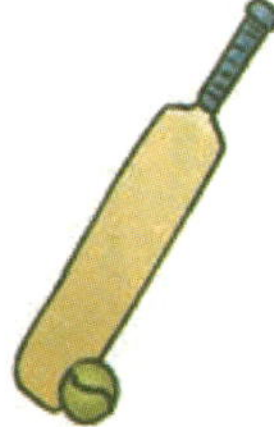

3. need
4. want

5. need
6. want

7. need
8. want

WE LIVE IN A NEIGHBOURHOOD

Look at the drawing of Nancy's neighbourhood and fill in the blanks.

A neighbourhood is a place where people live. Every neighbourhood has homes, school, shops and other places.

Sterling Apartments
Park
Bus stop
Grocery store
Cleaner's shop
Hardware shop
Dau Cleaners

1. Nancy's neighbourhood has a ______________, ________________, park, ______________ and ______________.
2. Nancy lives in ________________________.
3. ____________ is to the left of Nancy's apartments.
4. Nancy and her friends play in the ________________.
5. Her neighbourhood belongs to a ________________.

COMMUNITY

A community is a place where people live and work together for the common good. There are three types of communities – urban, suburban and rural.

- Many people live close together
- Small amount of space
- Less open areas or natural areas
- Tall skyscrapers

- Close to, but not, in cities
- Fewer people
- Small apartments but no Skyscrapers

- Fewer people
- A few buildings spread over large distances
- Lots of open space and natural areas

Try this!

Make a comparison chart to show things that are similar and different in urban, suburban and rural areas.

MY COMMUNITY

Answer these questions about your community.

1. What is the name of your community?____________________
2. Where is it located?______________________________
3. Which large city is it near?__________________________
4. Are there any historical monuments? If so, name them and state where are they located.

   a. ____

   b. ____
5. What is unique about your community?

   a. ____

   b. ____
6. Why do you like your community?

   a. ____

   b. ____

Draw a picture of the community you live in. Write a sentence to describe it.

GOODS AND SERVICES IN A COMMUNITY

Goods are things that people make or grow.

For example: crops, soap, jute bags

Services are jobs or work that other people do for you.

For example: a barber cuts hair, so he provides us a service.

Goods
apples for sale

Service
a barber cutting hair

Write goods or services for the pictures given below..

______ ______ ______

______ ______ ______

HELP!

There are many community services that help you in different ways. Which one should you call for each problem below?

Draw a line to match the need with the place that meets it.

1. You need help finding a fact for your science homework.
2. You see a fire out of your window.
3. You find a lost bag on the street.
4. You want to use the park for your cricket team party.
5. Someone has been hurt.
6. You need to find a zip code.
7. You see a leaking water pipe in your locality.
8. The garbage in your neighbourhood has not been picked up for 3 days.
9. There is a dangerous dog straying in your neighbourhood.
10. The electricity has gone out on your street.

Try this!

It is Saturday and Norman has a lot to do today. He has to go to the library to find a book about transport. Then he has to go to the clinic to get medicine for Granny. Next, he has to buy some postage stamps for his Mom. Lastly, for his Dad, he has to find out what time the soccer game starts. Name all the services Norman would use.

RULES IN A COMMUNITY

Just as we have rules in the family, we need to follow certain rules and laws in our community to keep ourselves safe and peaceful.

Write agree or disagree for these rules in the community.

1. No talking in the library.

2. No driving while operating a mobile phone.

3. All owners of television sets must have a licence.

4. No littering in shopping malls.

5. Spitting chewing gum in public places.

6. Walk on the track in a park.

7. Ignore traffic signals if you are in a hurry.

8. No seat belts while driving.

9. Playing loud music in the neighbourhood.

10. Park your car anywhere in the market.

Think about it

You are walking around the supermarket and are very hungry so you pick up a bar of chocolate; you eat it and throw away the wrapper before you exit. Is this OK?

RULES IN A COMMUNITY

Look at the picture and talk to your friend about it.

1. Who has broken a rule in this picture?

____

2. What has the driver of the yellow car done that is wrong?

____

3. What do you think the traffic police officer should do?

____

Think about it

What should you do when you see someone breaking a rule in the school?

COMMUNITY SIGNS AND SYMBOLS

We see different signs and symbols around us. These signs and symbols keep us safe and also aware of the community.

Look at these signs and symbols. Write the name of each sign. Choose from the help box.

Help Box

Railroad crossing	Stop	Bike Route	Caution
Handicapped	No Pedestrian	Phone	No Bike
School crossing	Men	Women	Exit
Bus stop	Hospital	Emergency	Walk

PEOPLE COMMUNICATE

Communication means sending information from one person to another. Talking is the most common way of communicating that we all know.

We can also communicate by other ways such as:

writing letters

using signs and symbols

email

newspapers

books

postcard

telephone

radio

television

fax

music

advertisements

Think about it

Look at these words and sentences. We can tell someone all these things without talking. Take turns with your friend to show how we communicate each one.

1. Come here 2. No 3. Quiet 4. I am angry 5. Stop

PEOPLE COMMUNICATE

Look at the picture. How many different ways of communication can you find?

1. How many people are reading something?

____

2. What kind of reading can we do for fun?

____

3. What do we read every day to find what is happening in our city and country?

____

4. What kind of communication is the "wet paint"?

____

5. Name one warning sign you see in the picture.

____

PEOPLE COMMUNICATE

Tick the correct option in each sentence.

1. We get stamps from the **(newspaper office/post office)**.
2. **(Letters/ e-mails)** are sent through internet.
3. **(Telephone/Television)** is the fastest means of communication.
4. We can carry **(telephones/mobile phones)** with us.
5. A **(letter/television)** is a means of mass communication.
6. You can find lots of information on any subject in a **(postcard/book)**.
7. A **(e-mail/newspaper)** is a printed means of communication.

Pretend you are on holiday in a town that you have not been to before.

Write a postcard to your friend about everything you have seen and done.

USING TRANSPORTATION

We use different kinds of transport to get from one place to another and to move things from one place to another. There are many different kinds of transport. Most of us travel by land on roads, trains and footpaths. We also use roads and trains to transport things by land.

In each sentence below, cross the information that is wrong. Correct the sentences and rewrite them.

1. Thousands of years ago, man used to travel from one place to another using a car.

   ____

2. In rural areas, people usually travel by bullet trains.

   ____

3. Dogs were used to pull carts some years ago.

   ____

4. Things like coal, vehicles and goods are transported by passenger trains.

   ____

5. The fastest means of transportation is train.

   ____

6. A yacht is a ship that remains inside the water.

   ____

7. Trains run on steel tracks that are called cars.

8. A helicopter can carry large number of people.

   ____

MAPPING MY NEIGHBOURHOOD

A map is a drawing of a place. Maps can be drawn to represent a variety of information such as roads, directions, places and more.

A map has:

Big Island

a title
name given to the map

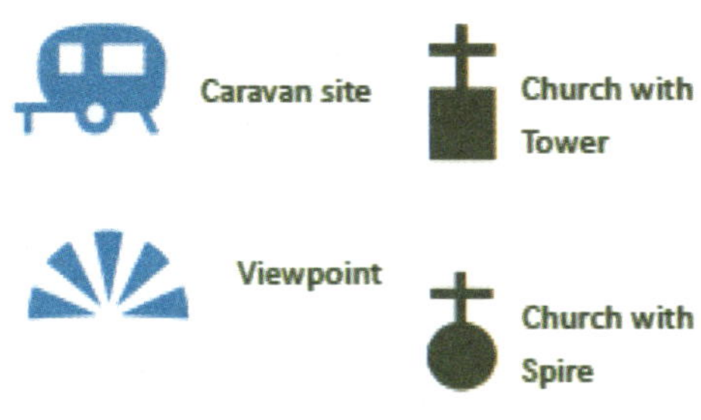

symbols
lines, shapes or colours

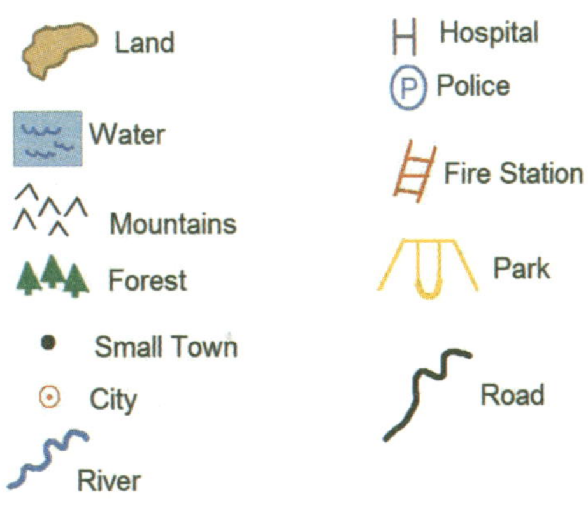

a legend or key
tell what the symbols mean

a compass rose
shows direction on a map

PICTURES AND MAPS

The model below shows Kate's community from an aeroplane. Study it and answer the questions.

Kate's Community

Circle the map that shows Kate's community..

Map A

Map B

Try this!

Look for pictures that show a community in an aerial view,
Can you identify houses and other places in the community?

PICTURES AND MAPS

Polly and her friends are playing hide and seek. Help her find her friends by looking at the map. Answer the questions.

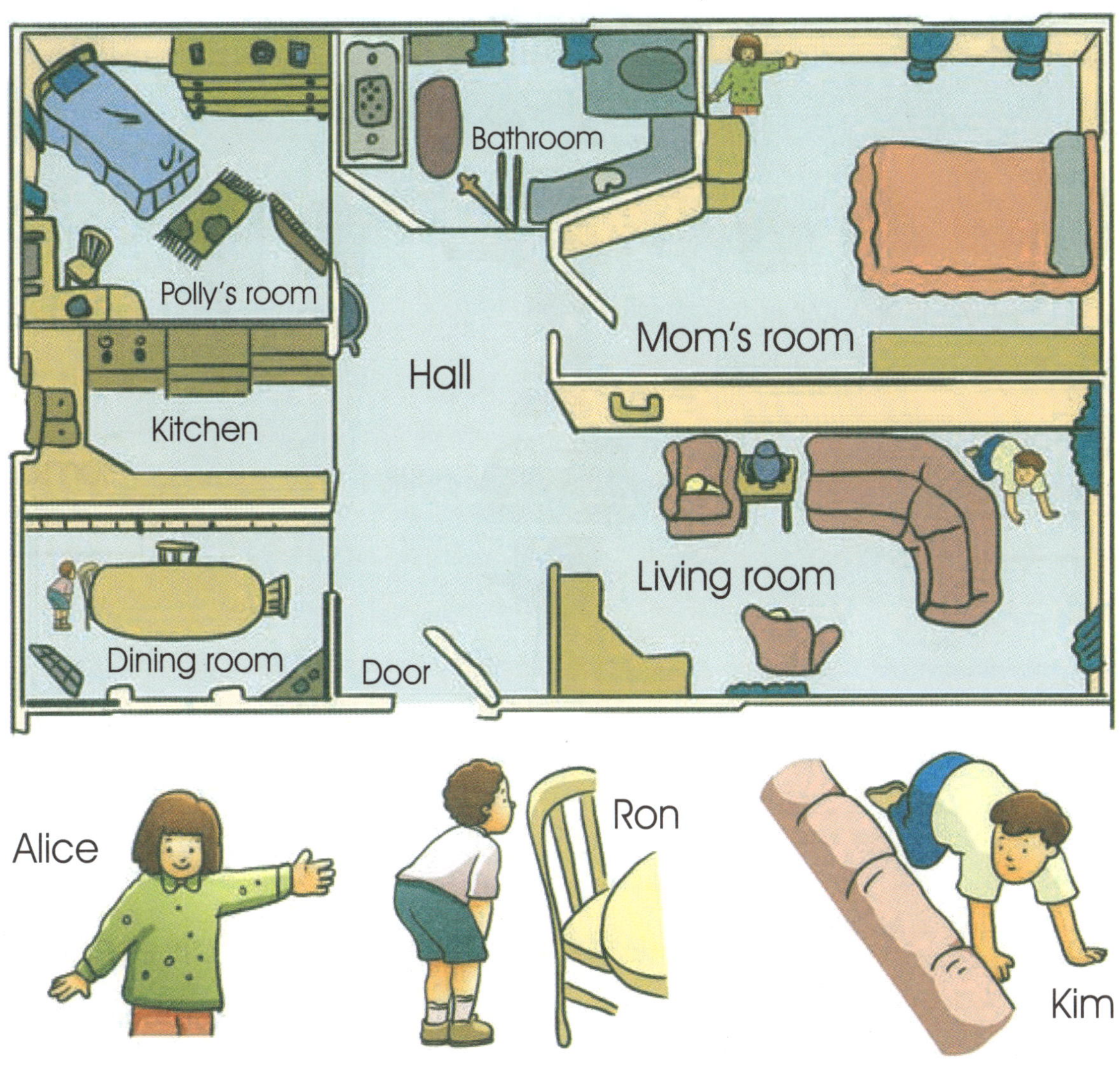

1. Where is Alice hiding? ______________________
2. Who is in the dining room? ______________________
3. Who is hiding in the room next to Mom's room? ________________
4. Where is Polly's room? Circle it. ______________________
5. How many rooms does Polly's house have? ____________________

FINDING DIRECTIONS ON A MAP

Look at the picture and answer the questions.

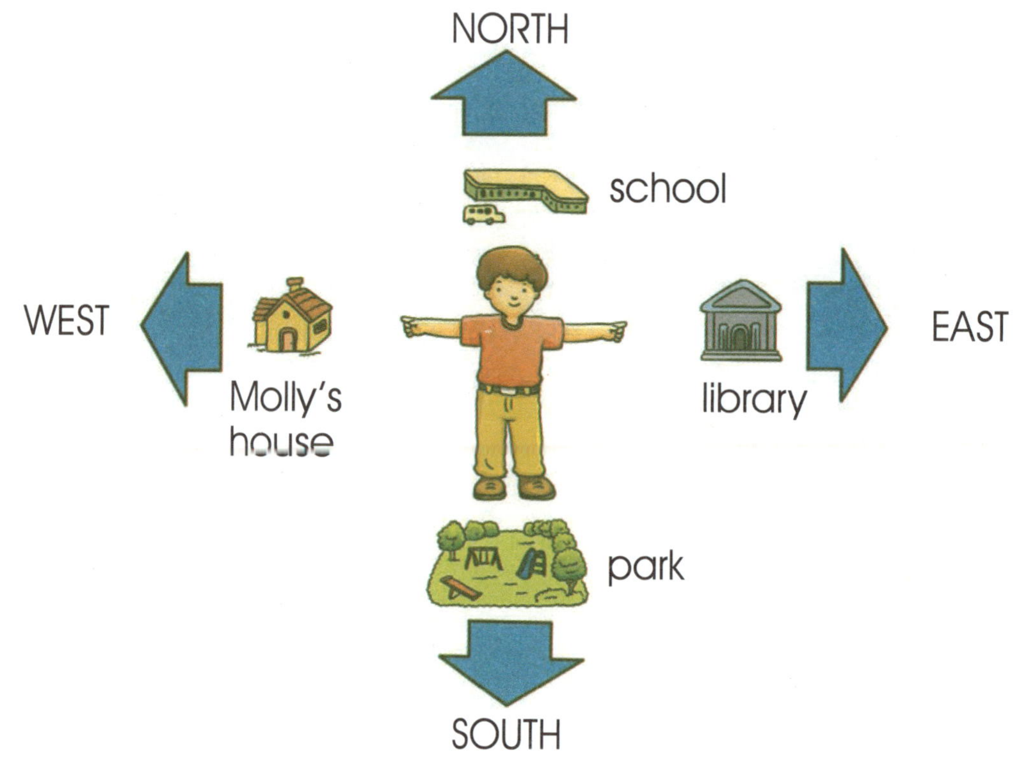

1. Name the four directions you see on the map.

 ____

2. In which direction should Daniel walk to go to school?

 ____

3. In which direction is the library?

 ____

4. Daniel wants to go to the park. In which direction should he move?

 ____

5. Molly's house is to the ______________ of Daniel.

Try this! Stand in front of your house facing the north. Name the places that are to your east, west and south.

MAP OF THE ZOO

Look at the map of the zoo. Then answer the questions.

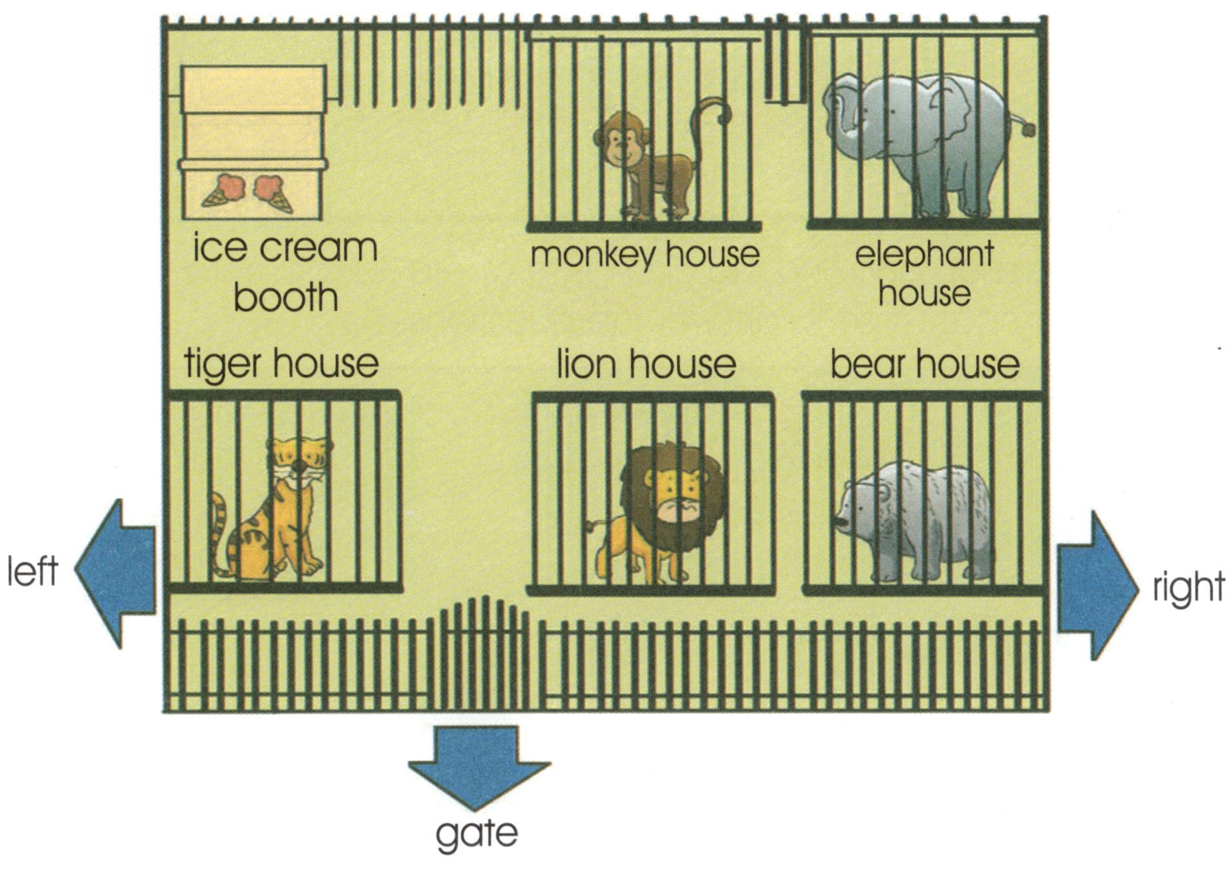

1. Which house is to the right of the ice cream booth?

____

2. Which house is to the left of lion's house?

____

3. Which house is to the right of monkey's house?

____

4. How many houses are to the right of tiger's house?

____

5. If you stand where the bear is, which house would be to your right and left?

____

USING A COMPASS ROSE

A compass rose is a figure on a compass, map, chart or monument used to show directions: North, East, South and West.

Compass rose

Look at the map and find the campsite where Jacob is staying. Then use the compass rose to answer the questions.

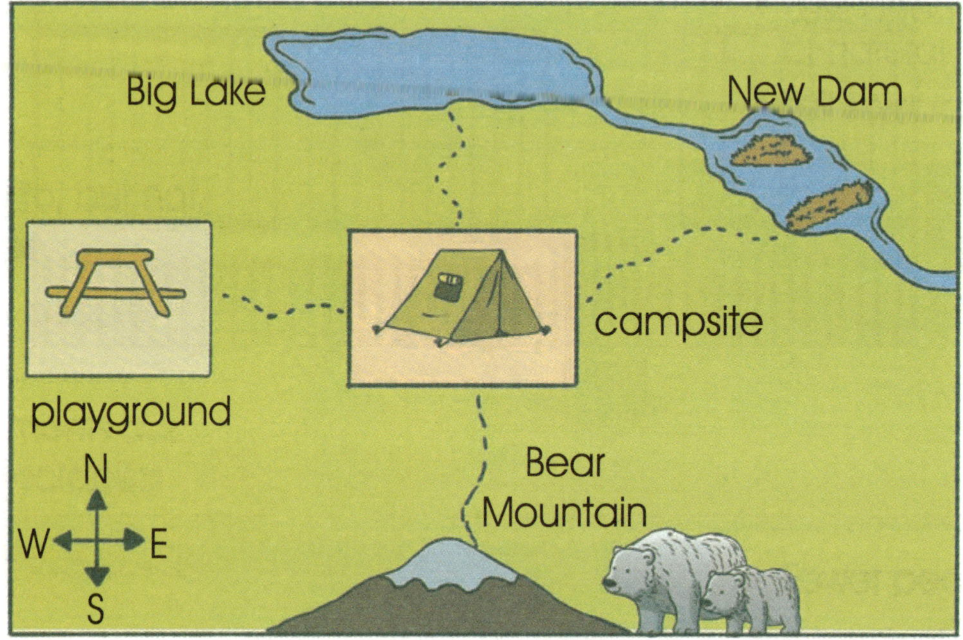

1. In which direction should Jacob walk to reach the playground?

____

2. Is the Bear Mountain to the west or south of the campsite?

____

3. In which direction should Jacob walk to reach the Big Lake?

____

4. Is the New Dam east or west of the Big Lake?

____

USING MAP SYMBOLS

Look at the map of a community below. Use the map and map symbols to answer the questions.

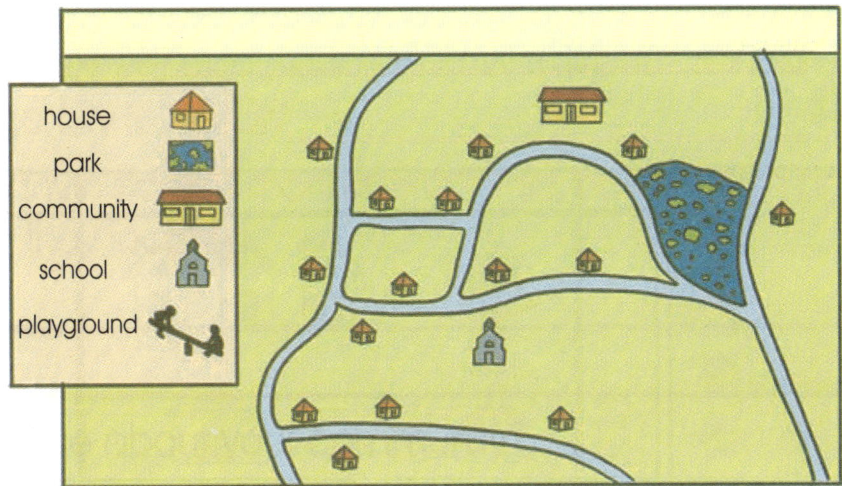

1. There are many houses in the community. Which symbol stands for a house?

2. What is to the east of the park? Circle it on the map.

____

3. What is the symbol of the community centre? Draw it here.

____

4. How many schools do you see on the map? Put a (✓) on the map.

____

5. Which symbol shows the playground?

Try this!

Draw a line to show the route you can take to reach the school from the community centre. Which directions you moved in?

USING A MAP KEY

A map key helps to study the information needed for the map to make sense. It explains what symbols or colours on a map mean.

Look at the map key. Find the symbols and circle them. Then answer the questions.

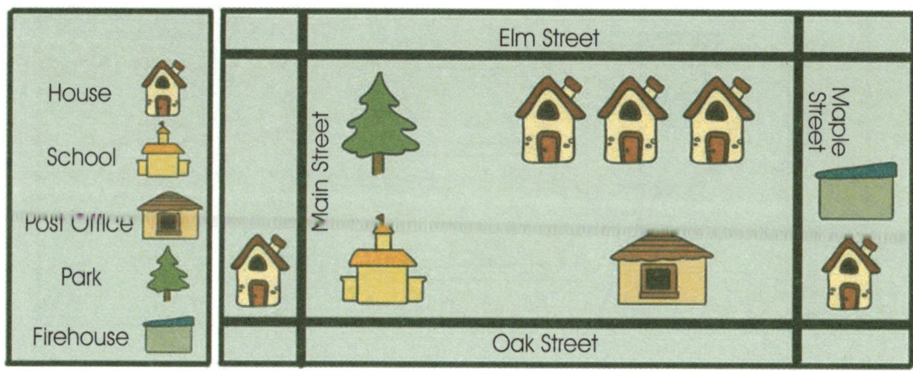

1. Which symbol stands for the park?

2. Which symbol stands for the firehouse?

3. How many houses can you see on the map?

____

4. Name the streets on the map.

____

5. Find the post office on the map and circle it.

Make a map showing any 5 places around your neighbourhood. Use your own symbols and key.

STUDYING A MAP

Look at the map carefully. Then answer the questions.

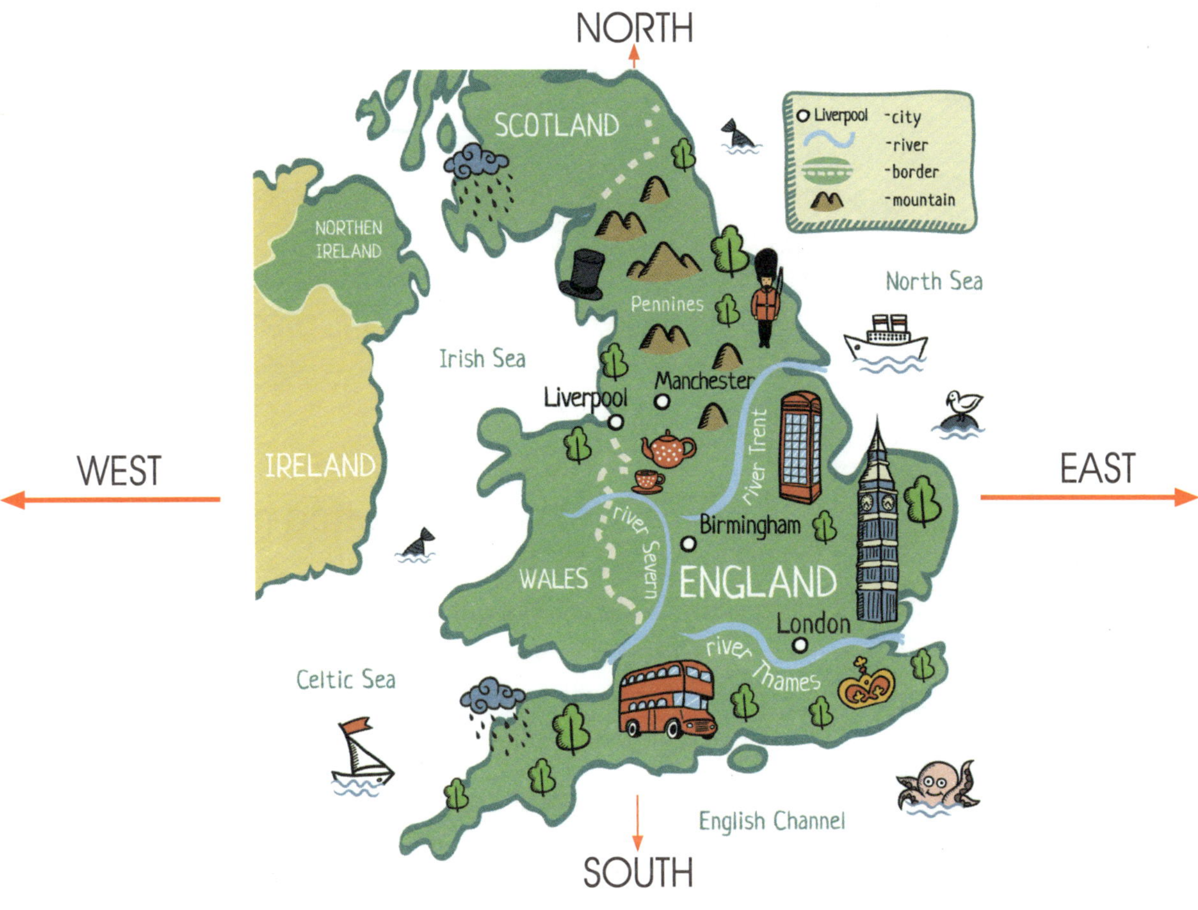

1. Which seas are to the west of England?

____

2. In which direction is Scotland from England?

____

3. In which direction should you move from Ireland to go to England?

____

4. Draw the symbols that show the mountains and rivers.

____

5. How many rivers do you see on the map? Name them.

____

LANDFORMS AND WATER

A landform is a natural feature of the Earth's surface.

River | Mountain | Hill | Pond | Desert | Coast | Lake | Plain | Valley | Ocean

Try this!

How are a mountain, a hill and a valley different from one another?

LANDFORMS AND WATER

Look at the drawing of different landforms and write the word used to describe:

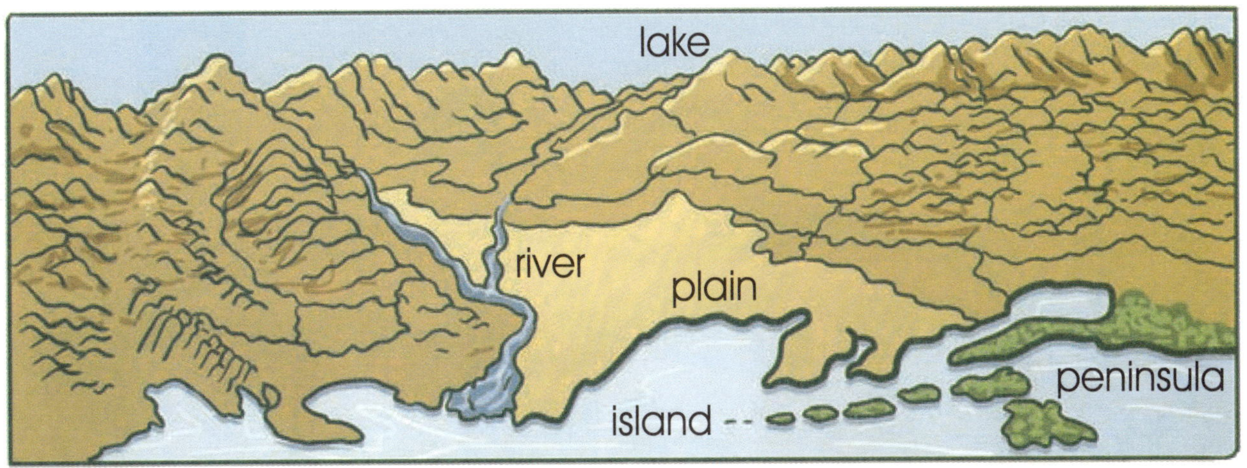

1. An area of land with water all around it.

____

2. A water body with land all around it.

____

3. A flat land.

____

4. A large natural stream of water flowing in a channel to the sea.

____

5. An area of land surrounded by water on three sides.

____

Try this! Use your own words to define: a desert, a pond, a coast

NATURAL RESOURCES

Natural resources are materials or substances occurring in nature which can be used by us.

For example: land, water, soil, sunlight

Look at the pictures. Put a tick on the natural resources.

TAKING CARE OF NATURAL RESOURCES

Tick the picture that shows ways to care for natural resources.

Throw litter on the ground

Throw litter in the trash can

Use things again

Take care of birds and animals

Help to keep the surroundings clean

SEEDS

A seed is a baby plant that has a bundle of food all wrapped in a pack.

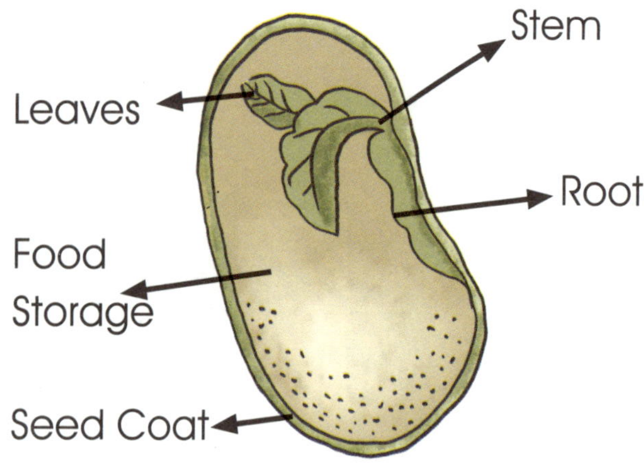

What does a seed look like? Seeds have many different shapes and sizes.

Marigold seeds are small and thin.

Star Anise

A pod is a shell for seeds. This pod has room for many seeds.

The peanut shell is hard and light brown.

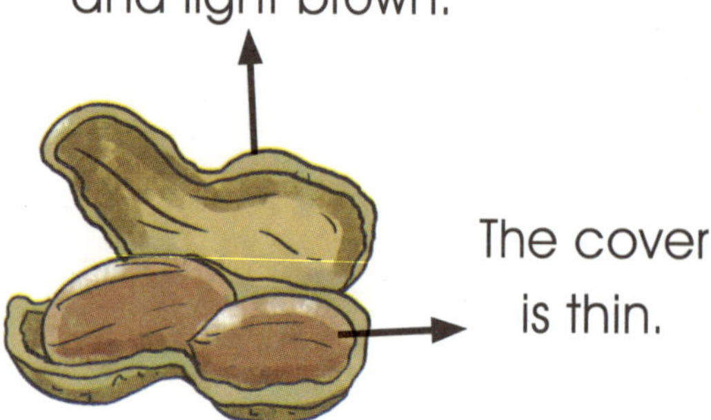

OBSERVE & INFER

Collect different seeds like wild rice, watermelon, lettuce, corn and other common ones and observe them. Make a chart to describe each one of them as shown here.

GROWING SEEDS

Seeds need water and air to sprout. When the seedling grows, it needs soil, water and sunlight to grow big and strong.

Draw a yellow sun. Draw blue water coming from a hose or watering can. Label the soil.

WHICH WAY DO I GROW?

Supplies:
glass jar with a screw lid
6 paper towels
water
2 green bean seeds
soaked in water overnight.

Directions:

Step1: Roll up six paper towels and place them in the glass jar.

Step2: Moisten the paper towels with water.

Step3: Insert two bean seeds between the paper towels and the glass so that each seed is visible from the outside of the jar as shown.

Step4: Place the jar in a warm, sunny area. In about three days, observe that roots begin to grow down from the seeds as shown. Keep the paper towels moist.

Step5: When the roots are about one inch long and a shoot begins to push out, screw the lid on tight and turn the jar upside down. Record your observations.

Number the pictures from 1 to 5 to show the growth of watermelon.

SEEDS SCATTER

To grow, seeds need to travel to new places in the ground. Here are some ways that they travel:

Some plants explode and send their seeds flying into the air.

Some seeds are light and have wings to travel on the wind.

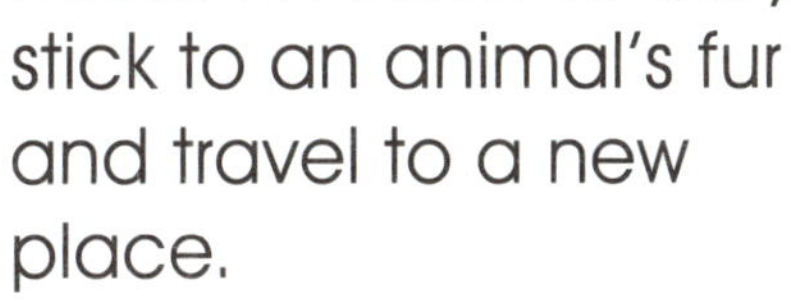

Some seeds have little hooks on them so they stick to an animal's fur and travel to a new place.

Some birds and animals can move seeds around and forget them in the ground.

Heavy seeds fall to the ground.

Many seeds are eaten by animals and are planted in their droppings.

Some seeds are hollow inside so that they can float on the water until they find a new place to grow.

Your turn

Find out how do these seeds travel:

blackberry, coconut, violet, wheat, dandelion, maple and sandbur

SEED PUZZLE

Read each clue. Write the missing word in the puzzle. Use the word bank.

Word Bank

wind
different
coconut
eat
food
parts
embryo
coat
protects
seeds
water
light
travel
sprout

Across

2. Every seed wears a seed____________.
5. Seeds can be____________shapes and sizes.
8. A partly formed plant is in a seed's____________.
10. Some seeds never____________.
12. Most people____________seeds every day.
13. A seed needs lots of____________to sprout.
14. The____________scatters some seeds.

Down

1. Every seed has three____________.
3. Most seeds do not need____________to sprout.
4. The seed coat____________a seed.
6. Seeds have their own____________.
7. A____________is a big seed.
9. Seeds____________in many different ways.
11. Plants make____________.

It is True

Most seeds remain dormant (asleep) until they are given water.

PLANT PARTS AND FUNCTIONS

Plants usually have branches, leaves, stems and roots. They bear flowers, fruits and seeds. Most plants have leaves that are green.

Tick the statements that are true for each part of the plant.

Roots:	**Stem:**
1. Fix the plant in the soil. 2. Carry water and minerals to other parts of the plant. 3. Some roots like carrot, turnip, radish and beetroot store food in them.	1. Gives support to the plants. 2. Carries water and nutrients from the roots to the leaves. 3. Leaves, flowers, buds and fruits grow on the stem.
Leaves: 1. Make manure for the plant. 2. Help the plant breathe. 3. Store food.	**Flowers:** 1. Make seeds. 2. Attract insects and birds. 3. Store food.

Label the parts of the plant.

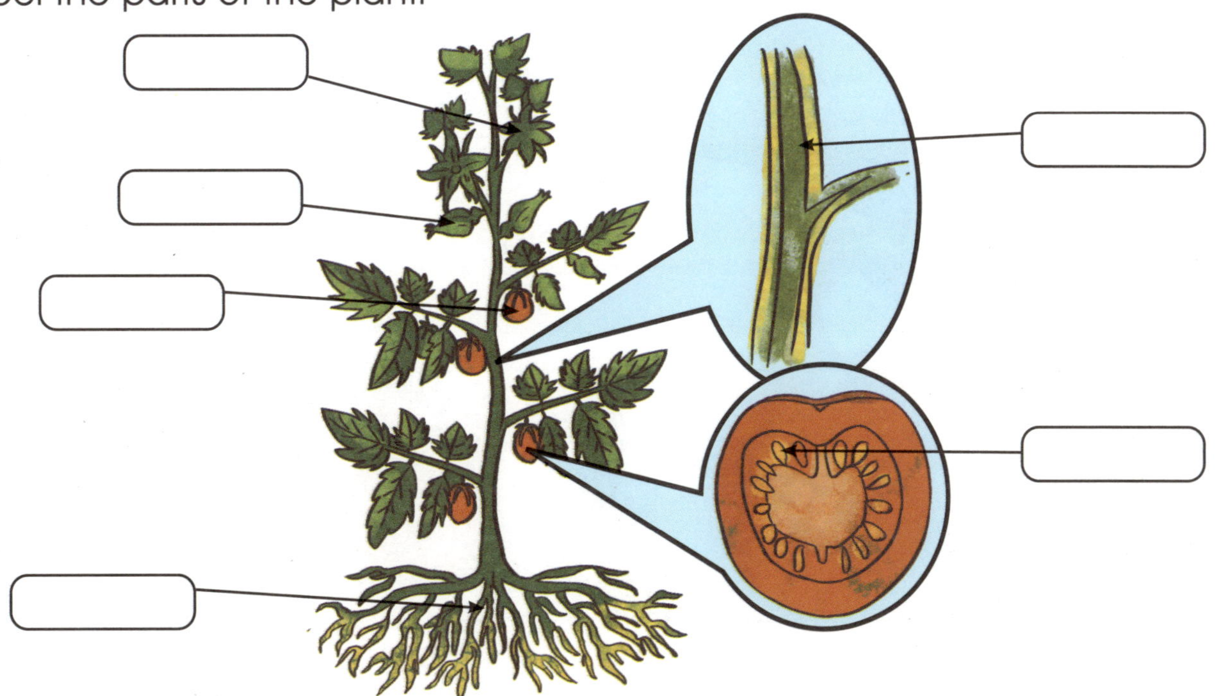

TYPES OF PLANTS

There are many different types of plants. Plants can be grouped according to the features they have in common.

Answer the riddles to find the names of different kinds of plants. Then choose the best example and look for the words in the word search.

1. I have thin woody stems and don't grow as tall as trees. _______ cotton/wheat
2. I have soft and green stems. I live only for a few months. _______ palm/mint
3. I am tall and strong with many branches. My fruits are hard on the outside but have water in it. _______ sunflower/coconut
4. I don't have strong stems so I crawl along the ground. _______ watermelon/grapevine
5. I need the support of another plant or sticks to stand. _______ maple/pea

W	W	M	I	N	T	L	V	Y	Y	Z	O	S	J	F
O	A	U	O	N	A	U	D	I	G	D	O	R	V	A
J	F	T	O	Q	W	A	T	E	R	M	E	L	O	N
L	V	Z	K	H	D	P	E	A	W	J	O	C	O	V
V	A	M	A	G	V	X	P	S	E	X	G	O	Q	I
I	G	R	F	I	F	T	W	H	N	N	J	T	V	B
X	W	H	W	C	O	C	O	N	U	T	T	J	H	G
T	L	U	C	L	E	S	H	D	U	Z	Q	N	M	X
Q	N	H	Y	B	L	P	H	L	E	K	E	S	V	T
X	Z	P	C	D	V	J	W	E	Y	H	Z	Q	Q	M
W	N	V	D	B	H	F	WA	H	K	E	N	H	W	Y
O	G	F	K	Q	T	H	C	J	Z	V	Y	U	G	R
J	I	Z	B	I	F	H	I	L	N	L	Q	D	J	M
Y	C	D	L	S	C	P	L	X	I	C	Z	R	T	K
O	K	J	D	C	O	T	T	O	N	A	P	J	F	D

FLOWERS AND FRUITS

Inside a flower is a sticky powder called **pollen**. Pollen helps flowers make seeds.

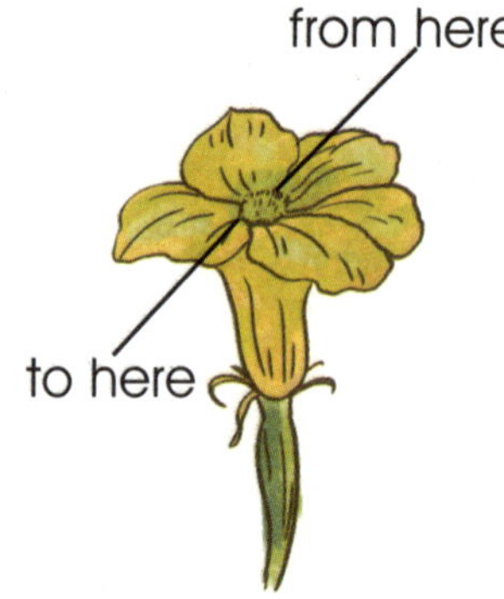

1. Pollen moves from one part of the flower to another.

2. The flower grows bigger and the petals fall off. It grows into a fruit.

3. The fruit protects the seeds inside.

4. When the fruit is ripe, it is ready to eat.

5. The seeds inside the fruit can grow into new plants.

Your turn

Find a plant to observe. Does the plant have flowers? Which sense did you use to find out?

ADAPTATIONS IN PLANTS

Plants have different ways to stay safe and get what they need.

For example:

The willow tree has long roots to get water from deep in the ground. A cactus has thorns to protect itself.

Look at each picture and write the special feature that each plant has.

It is True

It's not only animals that eat plants but some plants are hungry for animals too! The Venus Flytrap has leaves that shut when an insect lands on it. The leaves open when the insect is eaten up.

OBSERVE & INFER

Look for five plants and study the kind of special features they have. Make a table to record your observations. Then look for any bugs, brown or yellow spots on the leaves, curled leaves and stems or bark that looks like it has been chewed. Do these plants have any defence mechanism to protect themselves? How you do know?

INSECTS

Insects are tiny animals that are commonly seen in our surroundings.

Insect body has 3 main parts – head, thorax and abdomen

head

thorax

abdomen

Insects have 6 legs and 2 antennae.

Some insects live together in colonies.

All insects lay eggs.

Some insects may sting or bite you.

Insects use antennae to hear, touch and smell with.

Brain tilt

Which of these are not insects? Why?

butterfly	centipede	ant
earthworm	wasp	spider
dragonfly	termite	dog tick
lady bug	tapeworm	fly

It is true

Insects don't have bones. They have a hard covering called exoskeleton on the outside.

OBSERVE & INFER

Use the hand lens or microscope to look at a lady bug. What does it look like? What parts does it have? What do you think will happen if you touch the lady bug with the tip of a cotton swab? Gently touch the lady bug with the tip of a cotton swab. Describe what happened to the bug when you touched it with the cotton swab. Was your prediction correct?

HOW DO INSECTS GROW?

Complete the life cycle of the butterfly and fill in the blanks.

Insects start their life cycle as eggs. Their babies look totally different from them. The babies undergo amazing changes and grow to look just like their parents.

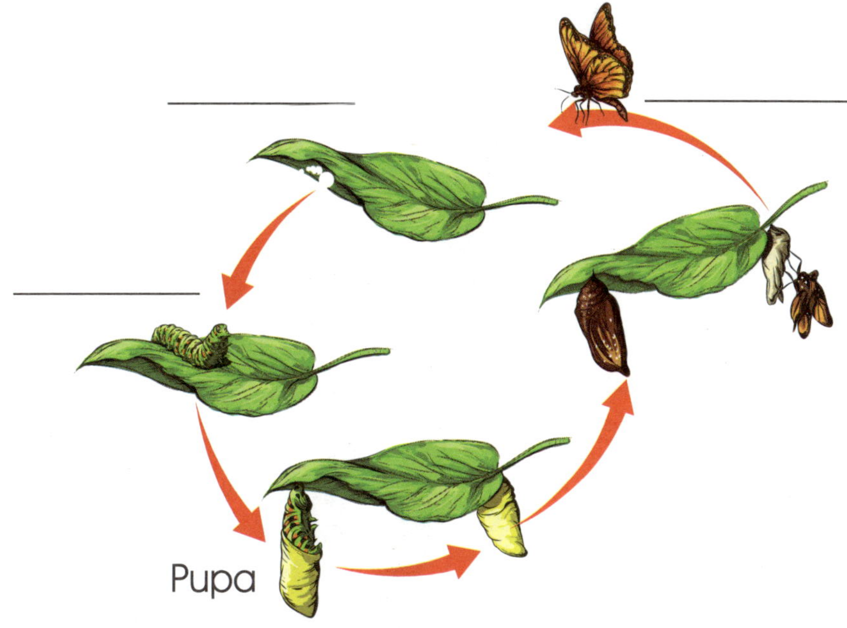

1. The butterfly lays eggs on a ____________.
2. The eggs hatch and ___________ comes out.
3. The larva is also called a ____________.
4. The larva sheds its _________ and begins to transform into a pupa.
5. After about _________ weeks, the pupa splits open and ________ comes out.

How do insects protect themselves?

Some insects __________ and __________ to protect themselves.

Some insects have _________ and _________ that blend with the hiding places.

Some insects taste _____ and so are not eaten by birds or other animals.

SPIDERS

Spiders are 8-legged animals with a two-part body. They are not insects but arachnids.

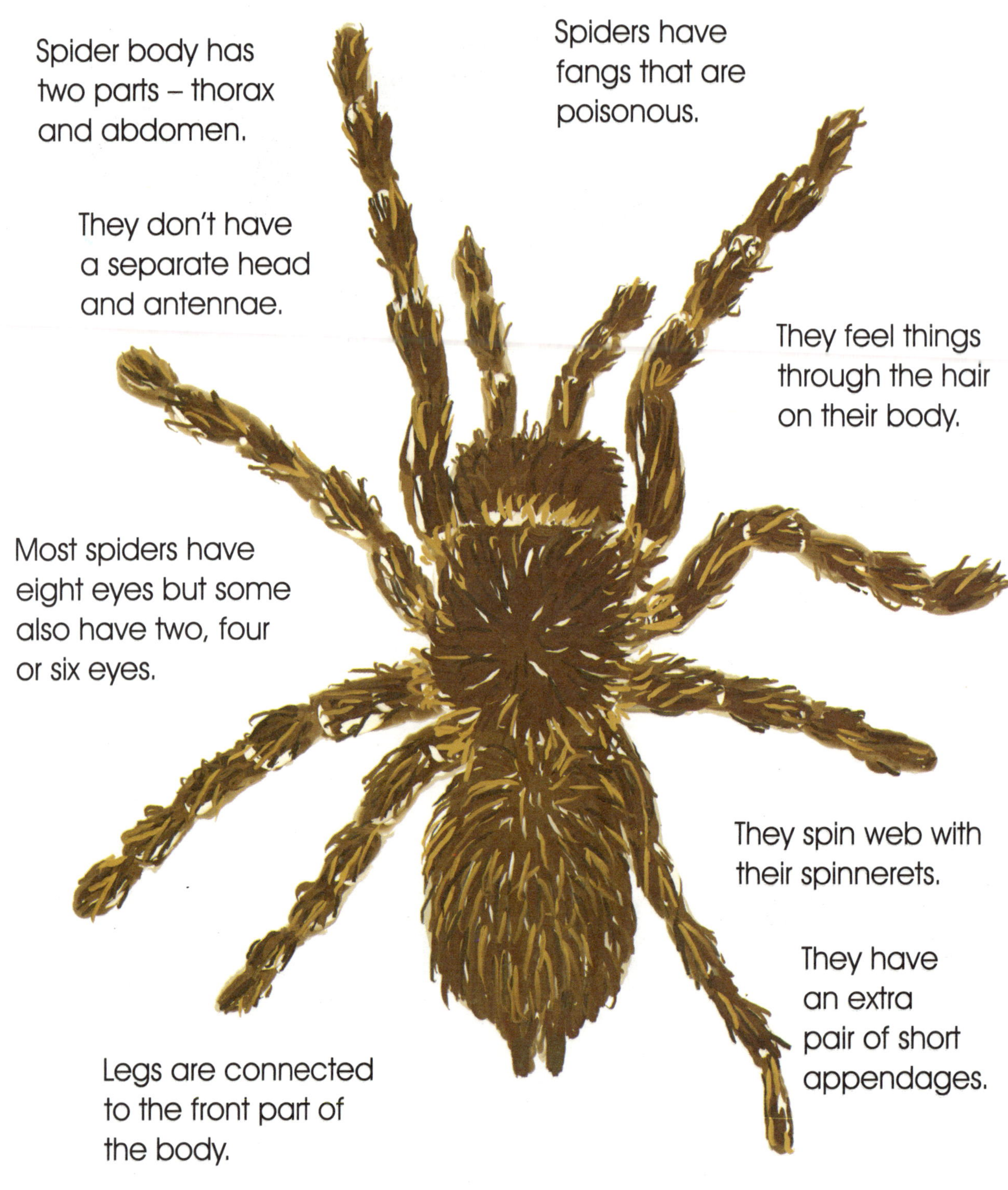

Complete the life cycle of a spider with the help of word bank.

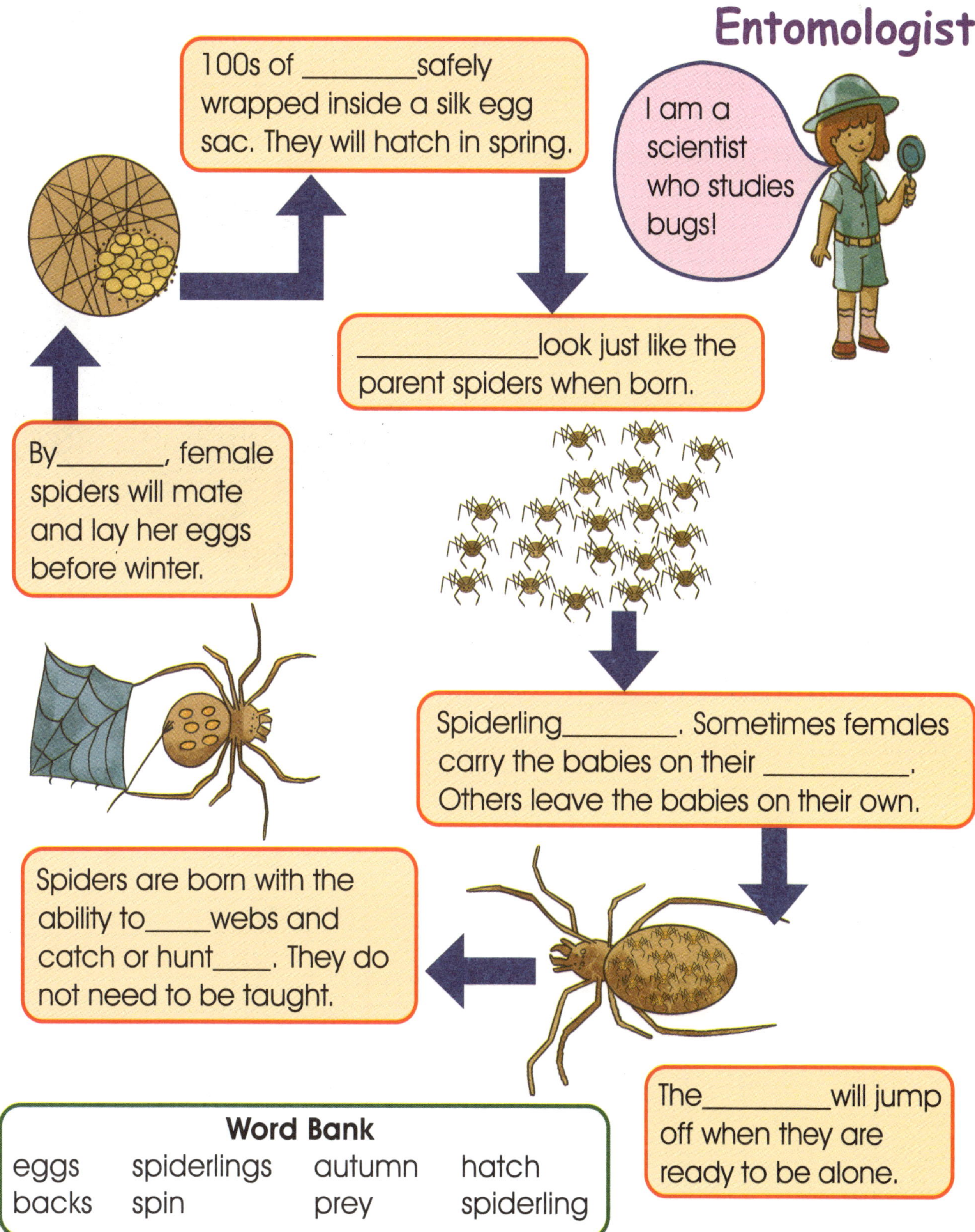

Word Bank

eggs	spiderlings	autumn	hatch
backs	spin	prey	spiderling

REPTILES

Find names of seven reptiles in the word search.

F	A	K	I	J	G	E	F	N	P	S	J	U	P	K
S	I	T	I	S	S	R	M	I	F	P	T	D	D	Q
N	Z	M	J	P	K	P	E	Q	E	M	O	P	D	S
A	T	J	Z	T	I	G	U	A	N	A	R	D	I	C
K	L	X	S	J	N	Q	Z	B	H	O	T	Q	N	R
E	M	I	A	O	K	D	O	O	D	S	O	U	O	O
V	W	E	X	I	Q	J	V	W	Z	X	I	H	S	C
B	T	R	E	C	A	Q	I	U	Y	B	S	L	A	O
N	Y	A	J	N	Z	D	J	G	O	F	E	T	U	D
K	W	N	W	I	I	V	Z	S	X	F	Z	B	R	I
X	Z	A	M	C	L	G	Y	W	C	K	M	S	H	L
V	L	Q	Z	Z	C	H	A	M	E	L	E	O	N	E
K	Q	L	R	J	U	G	D	W	J	K	Q	G	M	A
R	X	N	O	D	A	L	L	I	G	A	T	O	R	V
V	P	Z	L	I	Z	A	R	D	V	D	K	Q	S	B

Write True or False.

1. Reptiles are warm-blooded animals. _____
2. Reptiles have scales on their body. ______
3. Most reptiles shed their skin. _______
4. Reptiles are vertebrates so they do not have bones. _______
5. Most reptiles lay eggs. ______

OBSERVE & INFER

Study about different reptiles and find:
How they are adapted to live in their habitat
What they do when it's extremely cold.
How they keep themselves safe.
Do they blend into their environment?
Form a report.

It is True

Reptiles are cold-blooded animals which means their body temperature changes according to their surroundings. When it is warm outside they are warm and become cold when it is cold.

Complete the information about the reptiles below.

Snakes:

- Have ________ legs.
- Have a ________ sense of smell.
- ________ their skin.
- Shoot ________ or venom from their ________ into their prey to kill it.

Lizards:

- Move by ________.
- Eat ________, ________ and ________.
- Defend themselves by ________ when they are attacked.

Tortoises:

- Are the only reptiles with ________.
- Lay their eggs on ________.
- Eat ________.
- Pull their ________ and ________ into its shell when attacked.

Alligator vs Crocodile

Can you find the difference between a crocodile and an alligator? Well look at their snout and teeth. An alligator's snout is wider than a crocodile's. A crocodile has a pair of bottom teeth that show off even when its mouth is closed.

Your turn

Why doesn't a lizard fall off even while it is crawling on the ceiling? Find.

AMPHIBIANS

Amphibians are animals that:

- are cold-blooded
- have backbones and webbed feet
- breathe through lungs as adults and gills as young ones
- have moist smooth skin (no hair, fur or scales)
- live part of their lives in water and on land
- lay many eggs

Complete the life cycle of a frog.

Word Bank

jelly
adult
froglet
gills
legs
frog

OBSERVE & INFER

Study about different characteristics of amphibians and reptiles. Make a comparison chart to show how they are alike and how they are different?

BIRDS

Birds have many unique features which are different from other animals.

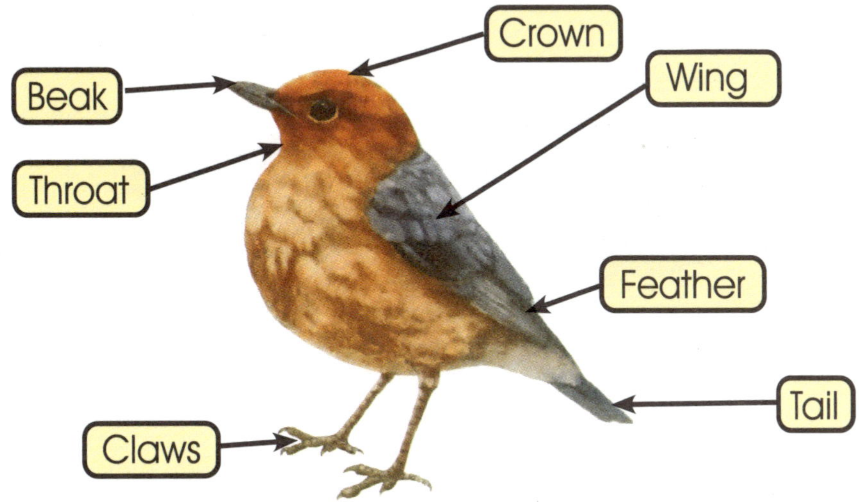

Fill in the blanks to complete the information about birds.

Birds:

1. have ____________ on their bodies.
2. fly with the help of their ____________.
3. have ____________ muscles that help them to move their wings.
4. have a ____________ shaped body that helps them to cut through the air.
5. have a ____________ but no teeth.
6. have a light body because of ____________ bones. This helps them to ____________ easily.

Birds have different kinds of feet that help them to swim, wade and perch. Look at the feet of different birds. Give examples of birds with such feet. Some have been done for you.

BIRD BEAKS

Look at the picture and write the kind of beak each bird has. Take help of the word bank.

1. ____________

2. ____________

3. ____________

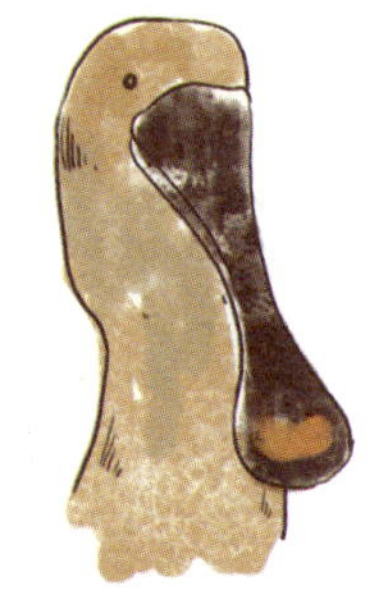

4. ____________

5. ____________

6. ____________

7. ____________

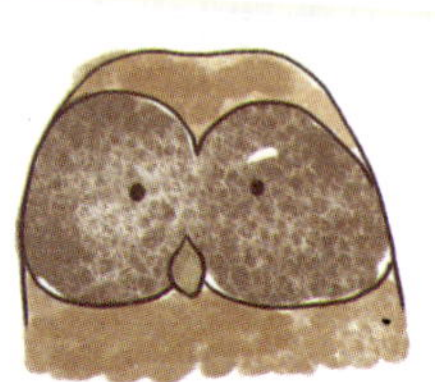

8. ____________

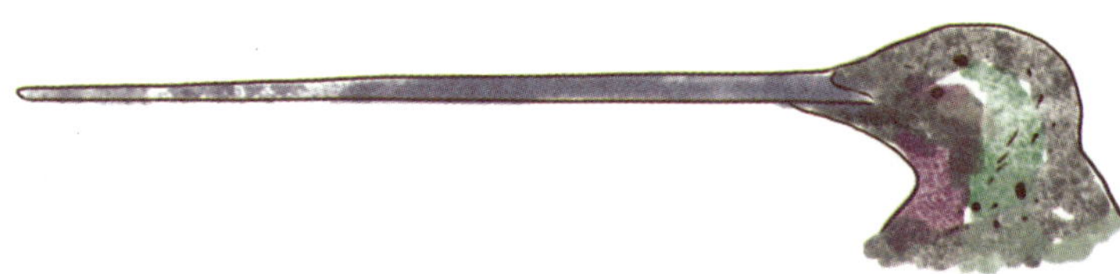

9. ____________

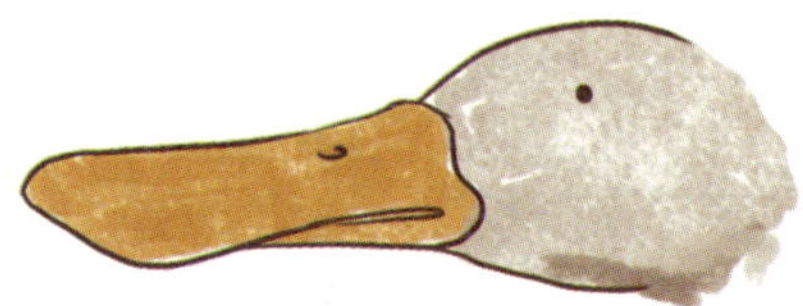

10. ____________

Word Bank

small conical beak	long slender beak	hooked beak	slender
curved beak	slender beak	spatulate beak	sharp
beak	short curved and downward-facing beak		

MAMMALS

Mammals are animals that give birth to their young ones. They have hair or fur on their body. Mammal mothers nurse their young ones with milk. Mammals are warm-blooded, that means, they can maintain their body temperature.

Solve the riddles to find the names of mammals in the Word Search.

1. I'm very, very big. I like to eat peanuts and hay.
2. I live in the ocean. I sing to my family and can breathe through a hole on the top of my head.
3. I have four legs. I like to smell things. I wag my tail when I am happy.
4. I'm very big and furry. I like to go on a sleep when winter is on a hurry.
5. I like to use my long tongue to eat leaves from tops of trees. I don't have to climb up though. With my long neck it's a breeze.

WORD SEARCH

S	G	P	T	Z	A	K	J	W	W
E	Y	W	N	J	F	M	D	Q	N
J	K	K	K	K	V	Y	G	T	K
A	Y	S	G	G	V	P	O	A	S
C	B	P	U	X	U	I	N	B	X
Q	K	Q	Q	N	H	D	O	G	W
E	I	D	B	D	B	E	A	R	L
E	L	E	P	H	A	N	T	M	W
D	O	L	P	H	I	N	F	G	P
H	G	I	R	A	F	F	E	N	Q

WHAT DO MAMMALS EAT?

A mammal can be a carnivore, herbivore or omnivore.

Carnivore: an animal that eats flesh of other animals.

Herbivore: an animal that eats plants.

Omnivore: an animal that eats both plants and animals.

FISH

The body of fish is covered with scales and shiny coating. Fish reproduce by laying eggs.

PARTS OF A FISH

Fill in the blanks with the words from the word bank.

1. Most fish have __________ that cover their skin.
2. Scales help __________ fish.
3. Fish have special organs called ___________ located on the sides of their head.
4. Gills are made of thin sheets or ___________ and help the fish _____________.
5. The fins of a fish help it to swim, ________, stop and _________.
6. The __________ fin is used for swimming.

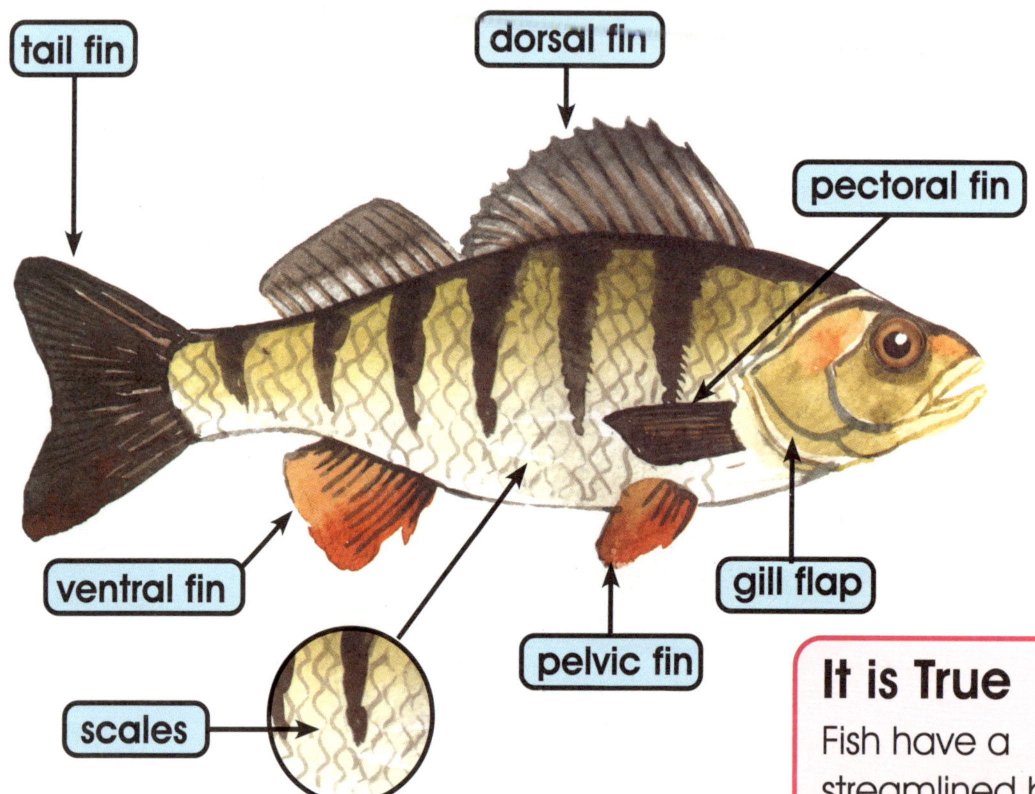

Word Bank			
steer	balance	gills	membranes
scales	protect	breathe	tail

It is True

Fish have a streamlined body i.e. pointed snout and rear. This helps the fish swim efficiently through the water.

WEATHER

Weather is the state of the atmosphere that tells if it is hot or cold, wet or dry, calm or stormy, clear or cloudy.

What makes weather?

There are many factors that make weather happen. Look at the picture below and write the names of the factors in the correct place.

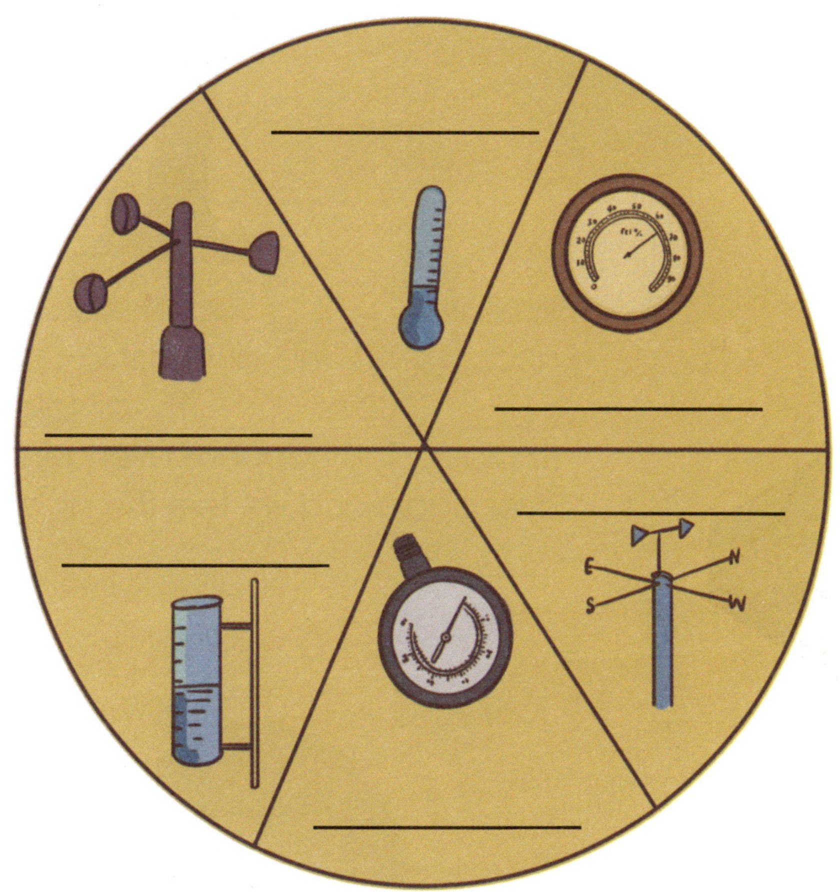

Word Bank

Pressure
Humidity
Temperature
Wind speed
Precipitation
Wind direction

Identify the instruments and write their names below.

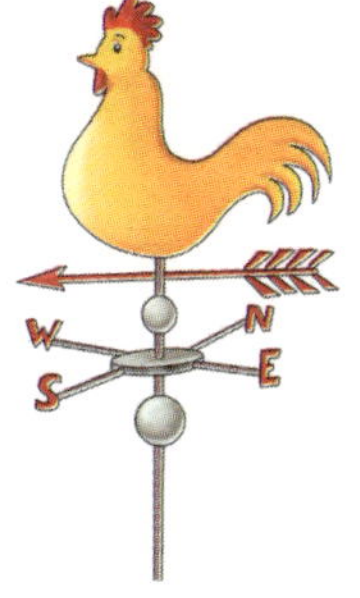

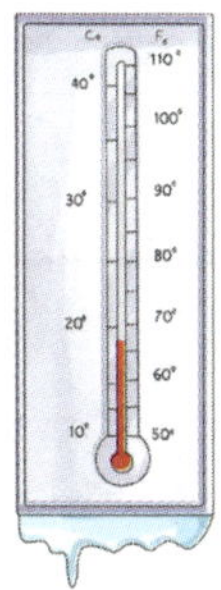

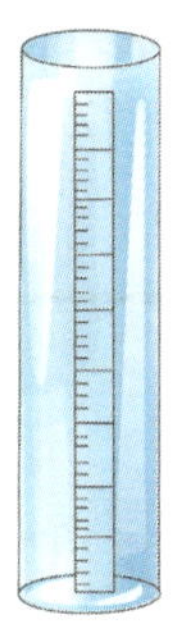

Fill in the blanks to complete the information about factors that make weather happen.

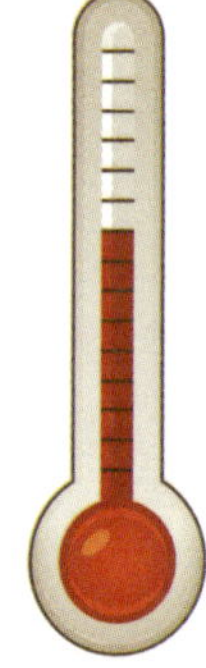

Temperature is how __________ or cold it is. We use a _____________ to measure temperature. The __________ the weather, the higher the liquid in a thermometer rises.

Wind is __________ air. The Sun's heat ____up the air and it ________ up. ___________ air takes its place. This happens over and over again and we feel the air as ________.

Humidity is the amount of _________ in the air. Water in the _________, seas, lakes and rivers is __________ by the Sun. Some of it evaporates and turns into a gas called ___________________________

Word Bank

cold	thermometer	moisture	weight
warmer	oceans	moving	hot
warms	wind	rises	heated

The __________ of air pushing on the earth is called air pressure.

MAGIC WATER GLASS

You will need

A glass

Water

Index card

What to do?

- Fill a glass one-third with water.
- Cover the mouth with an index card and invert (holding the card in place) over a sink.
- Remove your hand from the card.

What happened?

The card stays in place because air is heavier than water. The card stays in place because of air pressure. The air under the card pushes it strongly and keeps the card in place. The water pushes the card down but the air pressure is higher than the pressure of water!

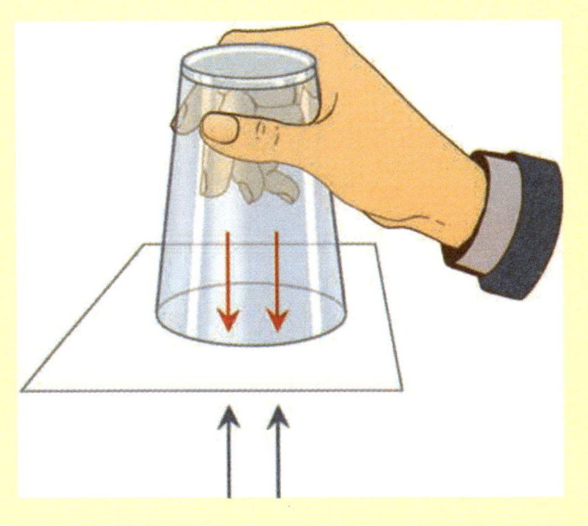

WATER CYCLE

The water on the earth keeps going around and around in a continuous cycle in what we call the "Water Cycle". In this cycle the water circulates between the Earth's oceans, atmosphere, and land, and returns to the atmosphere by evaporation and transpiration.

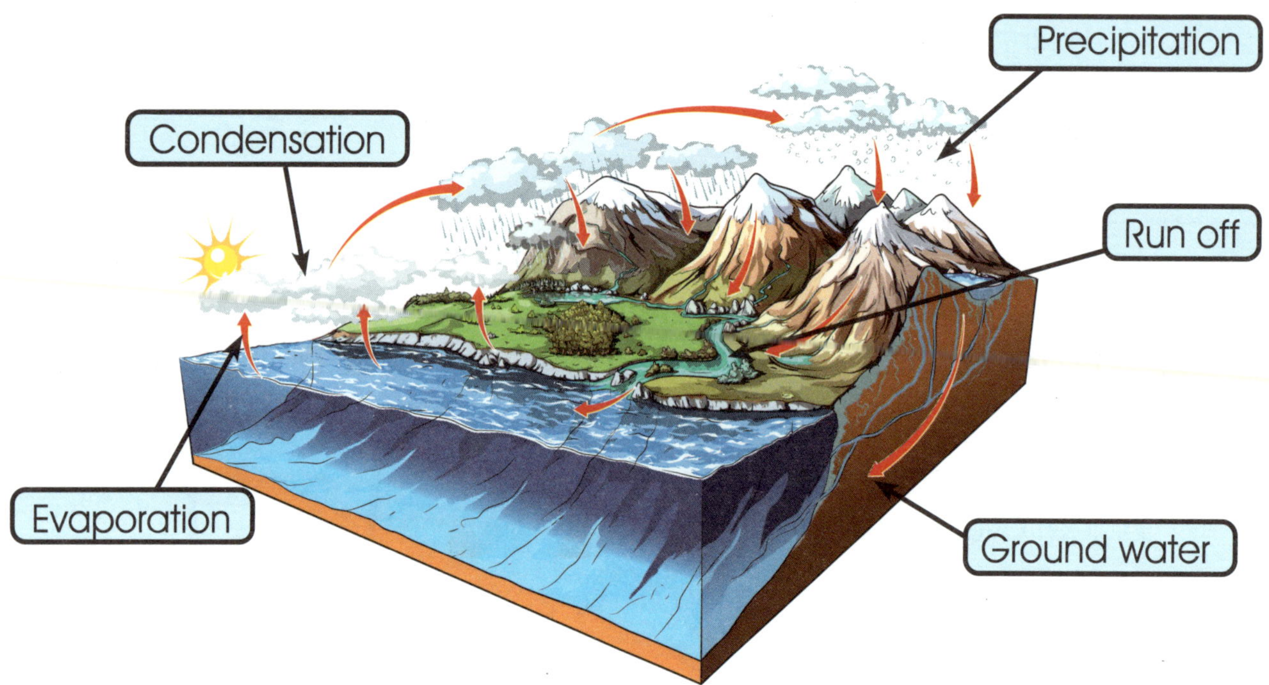

Match the label to the definition.

Evaporation	A change of phase from liquid to solid.
Transpiration	The process by which surface water enters the soil.
Condensation	A change of state from a liquid to a gas.
Precipitation	The loss of water from plants and vegetation.
Infiltration	The name given to condensed water vapour falling from the sky. Most occurs as rain, snow and hail.

FORCE

Force is a push or pull.

What can force do?

Force can change the state of motion of a moving body.

Force can move a body at rest.

It can sometimes change the size or shape of a body.

OBSERVE & INFER

Kick a football hard.
What type of force do you use?
Can you describe other sports or activities that involve push and pull?

LETTER QUIZ

Can you figure out the answers to these questions?

If you know the letters of the alphabet, this is going to be easy.

A	B	C	D	E	F	G	H	I	J	K	L	M
1	2	3	4	5	6	7	8	9	10	11	12	13
N	O	P	Q	R	S	T	U	V	W	X	Y	Z
14	15	16	17	18	19	20	21	22	23	24	25	26

Name a fruit that begins with the fourth vowel.

orange

Which letter sounds like the name of a body organ?

______

Which letter sounds like the name of an insect?

______

Which letter sounds like the name of a vegetable?

______

Which letter sounds like the name of a tool?

______

Which letter sounds like the name given to a group of people standing in a line?

______

RIDDLES WITH LETTERS

All these riddles have Jig confused. Help him solve them.

All the answers are five-letter words.

I walk on sand in the desert.

c	a	m	e	l

I am a vegetable that makes you cry.

I tell you what time it is.

I give you a lot of wool.

I am a red fruit.

You write with me on a blackboard.

SWEET AND SOUR

Complete the sentences by unscrambling the words and filling in the blanks.

Unscrambling can be fun!

I saw grapes (persga) growing on a __________ (ivne).

Their __________ (esnbuhc) are looking beautiful and nice.

Some are __________ (negre) and some are __________ (acblk).

Some are __________ (teswe) and some are __________ (rous).

Everyone loves to __________ (tea) them.

BUTTERFLIES IN THE SKY

Form words that begin with the letters on the butterflies.

How many words do you know?

ODD PICK

Tick (✓) the odd one out in the groups given below.

If you know which one doesn't fit, you will know which one to tick!

mango ◯ | potato ✓ | lychee ◯ | pear ◯

bus ◯ | car ◯ | boat ◯ | scooter ◯

oven ◯ | computer ◯ | laptop ◯ | tablet ◯

dog ◯ | cat ◯ | cow ◯ | tiger ◯

WHO'S IN THE WATER?

Jig went to the beach and saw something interesting. He has written a coded message about it. Can you decode it?

1	2	3	4	5	6	7	8	9	10	11	12	13	14	15
A	D	E	H	I	L	N	O	P	R	S	T	U	Y	W

4 13 10 10 1 14 | 5 | 11 1 15

H _ _ _ _ _ ! / _ / _ _ _

1 | 2 8 6 9 4 5 7 | 5 7

_ / _ _ _ _ _ _ _ / _ _

12 4 3 | 15 1 12 3 10

_ _ _ / _ _ _ _ _ .

PATTERN TIME

Can you complete these letter patterns?

ABC | CDE | DE_F_ | EFG | FGH

PP | __ __ | RR | SS | TT

IJ | KL | MN | __ __ | QR

__ __ | D4 | E5 | F6 | G7

ZY | XW | VU | TS | __ __

TREAT YOURSELF

Help Saw fill in the blanks with the correct words.

The words given in the box will help.

basket	scoop	glass	cup	slice	pack	bunch

Give me a ____slice____ of cake.

Give me a ________ of grapes.

Give me a ________ of biscuits.

Give me a ________ of tea.

Give me a ________ of milk.

Give me a ________ of fruits.

Give me a ________ of ice cream.

WHAT'S IN THE WORD?

Read the big words and find the smaller words in them.

A word with another word in it is called a kangaroo word.

catch

action

person

earth

ear

bold

island

history

WORD BOUQUET

Complete the word bouquet by finding smaller words from the bigger words.

garden — den

pastry — ______

balloon — ______

cartoon — ______

teacher — ______

swing — ______

SPELLING BEE

Are you a spelling bee? Prove it by writing the correct spellings.

Word	Correct spelling	Word	Correct spelling
plet	plate	truk	
forc		nale	
cyube		trane	
botel		horce	
blak		hypo	

CLIMB THE LADDER

Arrange the words in alphabetical order, starting from the top rung.

Sing the alphabet song as you sort the words.

rain	air
sunny	
cloudy	
air	
wind	wind

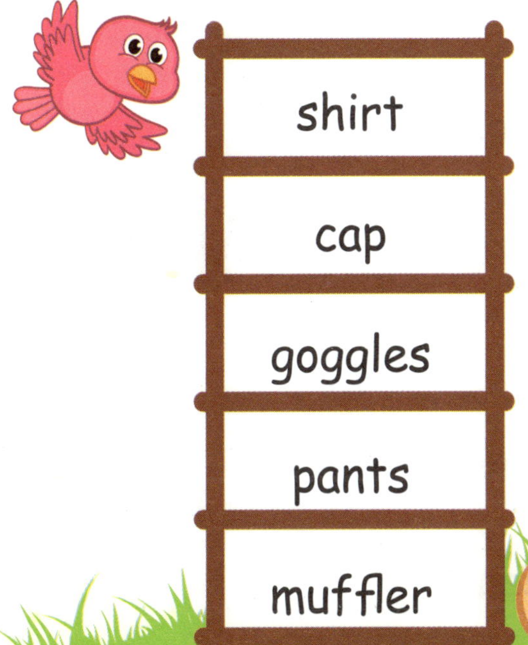

HOW ARE YOU?

Choose the right word from the options to complete these sentences.

The pictures hold the key!

I am a caring doctor.

smart caring greedy

I am a ________________ boy.

dry shiny smart

I am a ________________ fox.

brown black blue

I am a ________________ owl.

white brown green

I am a ______________ animal.

big small tiny

I am a ______________ soldier.

brave smart scared

I am a ______________ girl.

pretty big soft

I am a ______________ bird.

black colourful white

I am a ______________ animal.

short round tall

HE AND SHE

What is the opposite gender?
Fill in the boxes.

Identify and name them.

king | queen

father |

boy |

lion |

uncle |

hen |

284

WHAT'S THE MOOD?

These are pictures of Robbie with different expressions. Can you identify his mood in each?

Try to imitate Robbie's expressions.

He is crying.

He is ________.

He is ________.

He is ________.

He is ________.

He is ________.

SOUND POPS

Read the words in the balloons aloud. Colour the balloons pink if the words have the "s" sound and yellow if the words have the "k" sound.

Read the words aloud clearly and slowly to know what sounds they are producing.

lace

coat

palace

book

race

coin

mice

frock

cage

juice

face

LARGE IS BIG

Help Tina match the words that mean the same.

Can you use each pair in the same sentence? Challenge your friends!

damp •	• duty
quick •	• delete
rough •	• giant
pain •	• desire
crave •	• moist
erase •	• fast
job •	• ache
huge •	• harsh

HOT AND COLD

Pick out the opposite of the first word in each row by colouring the circle green.

You already know what opposites are.

difficult	hard	easy	little
little	young	heavy	big
hot	cold	warm	boiling
giant	tiny	huge	enormous
mute	quiet	silent	loud
evil	bad	wicked	nice
pretty	ugly	smart	beautiful

WORDY CLOUDS

Add "un-" or "dis-" to the beginning of each word to make a new word.

"Un-" and "dis-" are called prefixes. When prefixes are added to words, new words are formed. It is like magic, isn't it?

un + happy = unhappy

+ like =

+ equal =

+ respect =

+ kind =

+ honest =

WHO AM I?

Add -er/-or at the end of each word to form the name of an occupation.

"Er-" and "or-" are suffixes. Suffixes are added at the end of words to form new words.

act + or = actor

teach + _____ = _______________

paint + _____ = _______________

doct + _____ = _______________

sing + _____ = _______________

farm + _____ = _______________

SUPER SAIL

Tick (✓) the boat that you want to ride in.

Both the spellings are correct. But which one matches the clue?

This is an ice cream.

This stops a car.

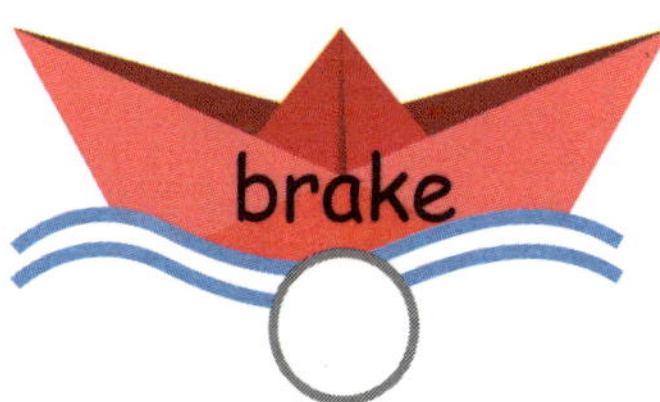

This is a grain.

This is a sweet dish.

The opposite of tight.

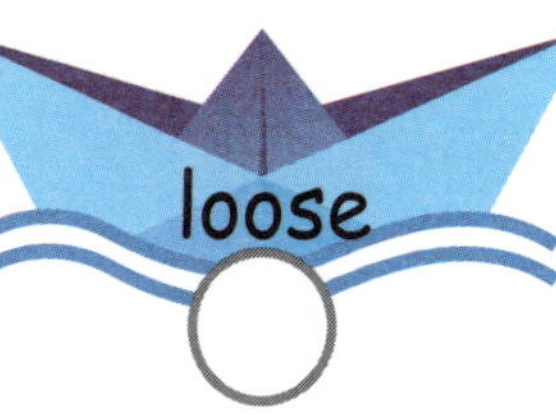

SENTENCE JUMBLE

All the sentences are jumbled. Help Jig set them right.

Always remember that a sentence begins with a capital letter and ends with a full stop.

sky	the	pilot	in	aeroplane	flies	the	an

The pilot flies an aeroplane in the sky.

breakfast	Rahul	bread	for	eats	butter	and

____

family	with	Tina	Kolkata	her	lives	in

____

doctor	My	is	father	a

____

going	I	picnic	am	tomorrow	a	for

____

BUILD A WORD

Saw is putting together bricks to form bigger words. Help her.

bull	water	back	air	ground
foot	suit	melon	pack	print
plane	play	case	dog	

water	melon		

TARGET SHOOTING

Cross the balloon with a word that does not rhyme with the others in the row.

Say the words aloud. If the ending sounds match, the words rhyme.

book	hook	cook	~~tooth~~	look
sleep	sheep	deep	deer	beep
draw	claw	paw	straw	bow
mug	buy	bug	tug	jug

SCRATCH YOUR BRAIN

Read the first word relation and select the correct word for the second one.

We use analogies to compare things.

child : teeth :: bird : beak

feather | beak | tail

gloves : hands :: socks : ____________

legs | feet | head

cherries : red :: pears : ____________

green | purple | white

eyes : see :: nose : ____________

hear | walk | smell

fire : hot :: ice : ____________

cold | warm | sweet

HUNGRY BUNNY

Circle the carrots that complete the analogies.

Put on your thinking cap.

Bricks make a wall, just as pages make a ____.

 car  map  book  bag

Plumbers repair taps, just as cobblers repair ____.

 bags  laptop  heater  shoes

Days make a week, just as months make a ____.

 hour  time   year  seconds

A triangle has three sides, just as a square has ____.

 five  four  two  six

Birds fly, just as fish ____.

 run  drink  swim  wash

KNOW YOUR SPORT

All these children are playing different sports. Do you know which one?

Do you know the names of different sports? Which one is your favourite?

b		d		i		t		

	o		k		y

f		o		b		l	l

	r		c		e	

GOOD MANNERS!

Help Saw learn some good manners.
Tick (✓) the right response.

Do you have good manners?

When your best friend gives you a gift, you say:

- Sorry ○
- Excuse me ○
- Thank you ✓
- Wow ○

When you meet someone, you say:

- Please ○
- Hello ○
- Sorry ○
- Thank you ○

When you disturb someone, you say:

- Sorry ○
- Thanks ○
- Excuse me ○
- May I? ○

When you ask for permission, you say:

- May I? ○
- Good-bye ○
- Hello ○
- Please ○

Answer Sheet

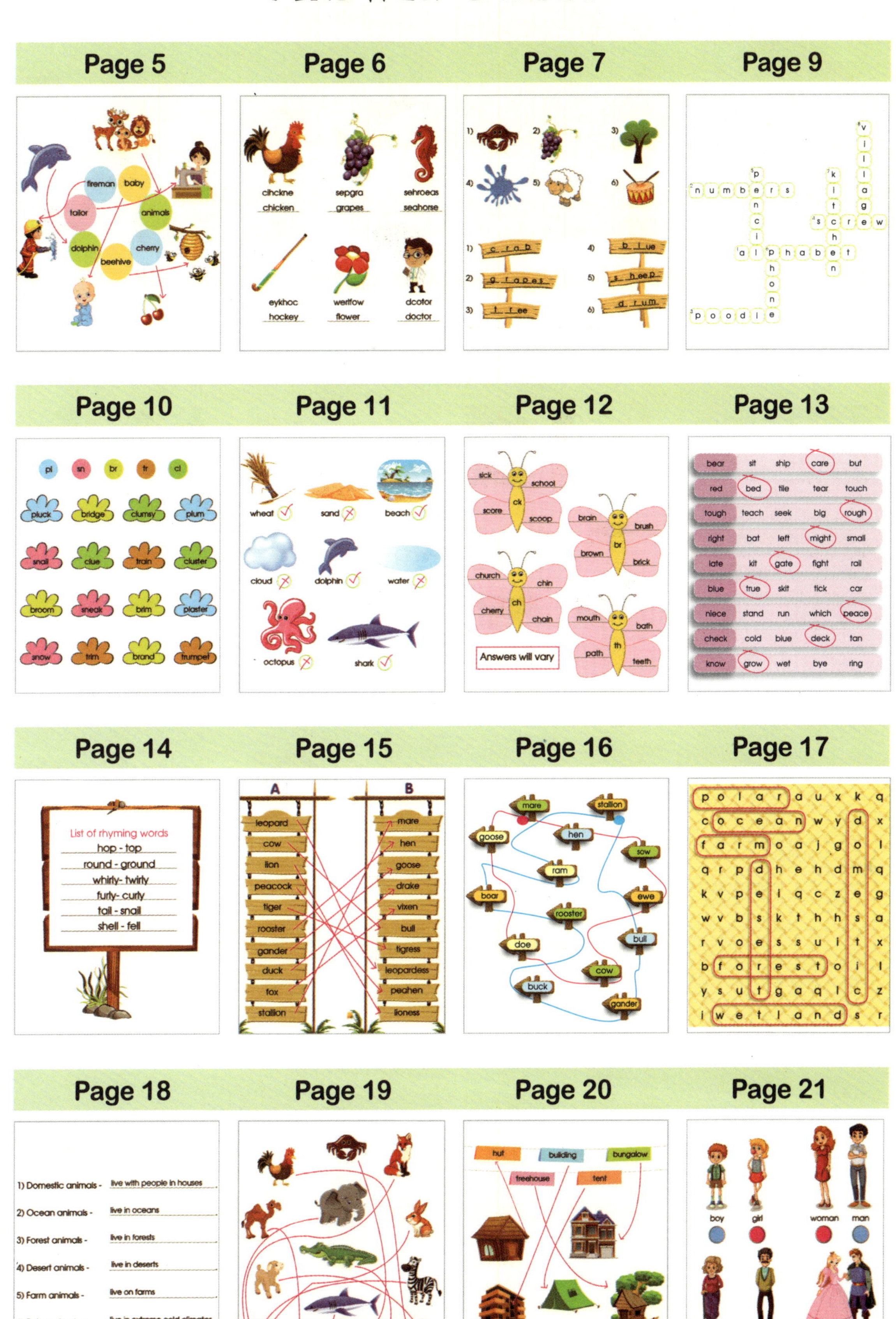

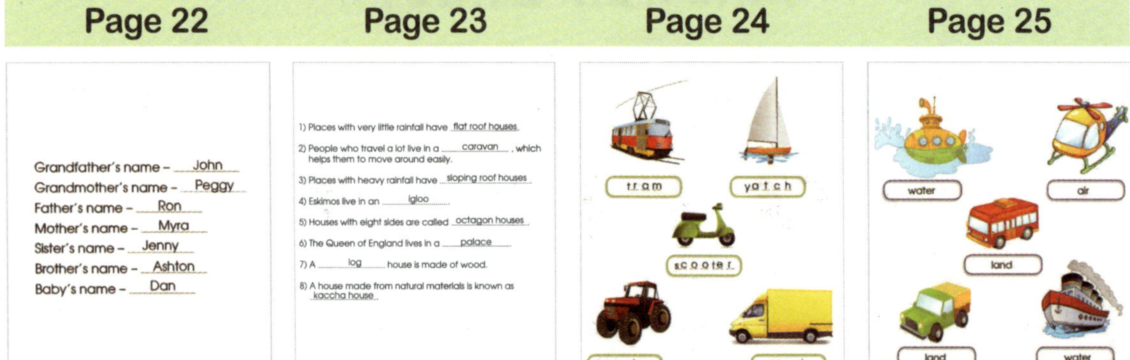
Page 22
Page 23
Page 24
Page 25
Grandfather's name - John
Grandmother's name - Peggy
Father's name - Ron
Mother's name - Myra
Sister's name - Jenny
Brother's name - Ashton
Baby's name - Dan
1) Places with very little rainfall have flat roof houses.
2) People who travel a lot live in a caravan, which helps them to move around easily.
3) Places with heavy rainfall have sloping roof houses
4) Eskimos live in an igloo.
5) Houses with eight sides are called octagon houses
6) The Queen of England lives in a palace
7) A log house is made of wood.
8) A house made from natural materials is known as kaccha house
tram
yatch
scooter
tractor
truck
water
air
land
land
water

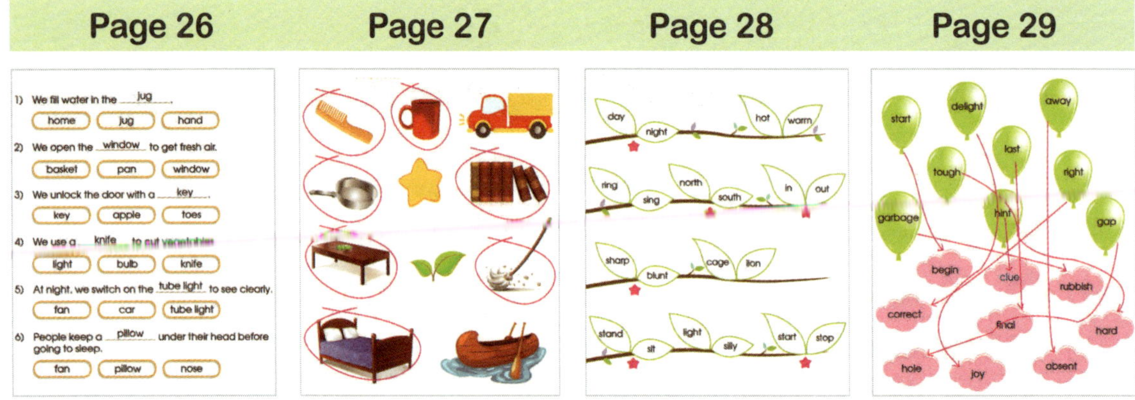
Page 26
Page 27
Page 28
Page 29
1) We fill water in the jug.
home jug hand
2) We open the window to get fresh air.
basket pan window
3) We unlock the door with a key.
key apple toes
4) We use a knife to cut vegetables
light bulb knife
5) At night, we switch on the tube light to see clearly.
fan car tube light
6) People keep a pillow under their head before going to sleep.
fan pillow nose
day night hot warm
ring sing north south in out
sharp blunt cage lion
stand sit light silly start stop
start delight away
last tough right
garbage hint gap
begin clue rubbish
correct final hard
hole joy absent

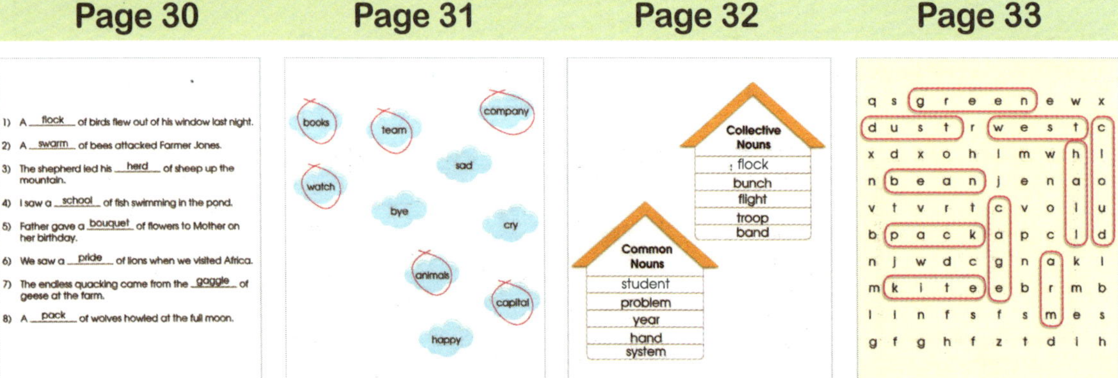
Page 30
Page 31
Page 32
Page 33
1) A flock of birds flew out of his window last night.
2) A swarm of bees attacked Farmer Jones.
3) The shepherd led his herd of sheep up the mountain.
4) I saw a school of fish swimming in the pond.
5) Father gave a bouquet of flowers to Mother on her birthday.
6) We saw a pride of lions when we visited Africa.
7) The endless quacking came from the gaggle of geese at the farm.
8) A pack of wolves howled at the full moon.
books team company
watch sad
bye cry
animals capital
happy
Collective Nouns
flock
bunch
flight
troop
band
Common Nouns
student
problem
year
hand
system
q s g r e e n e w x
d u s t r w e s t c
x d x o h l m w h l
n b e a n j e n a o
v t v r t c v o l u
b p a c k a p c l d
n j w d c g n a k l
m k i t e e b r m b
l l n f s f s m e s
g f g h f z t d l h

Page 34

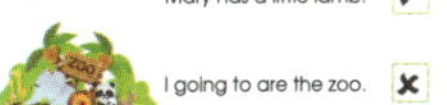

Cuckoos sweet sing. ✗

Mary has a little lamb. ✓

I going to are the zoo. ✗

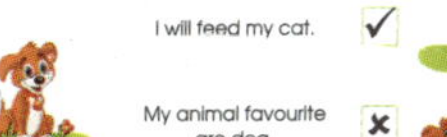

I will feed my cat. ✓

My animal favourite are dog. ✗

Camels are usually found in deserts. ✓

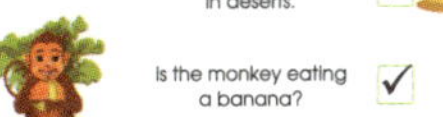

Is the monkey eating a banana? ✓

Page 35

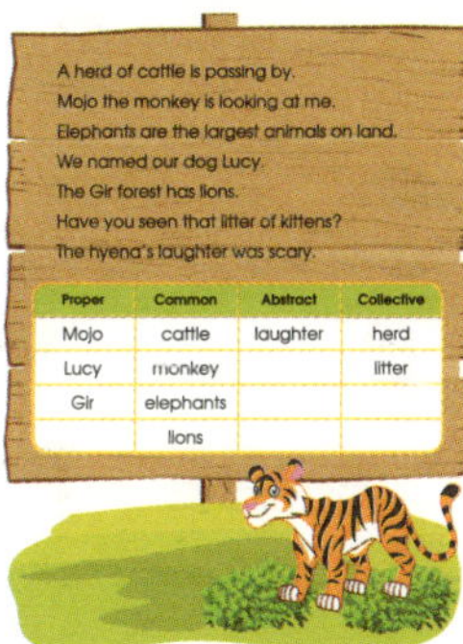

A herd of cattle is passing by.
Mojo the monkey is looking at me.
Elephants are the largest animals on land.
We named our dog Lucy.
The Gir forest has lions.
Have you seen that litter of kittens?
The hyena's laughter was scary.

Proper	Common	Abstract	Collective
Mojo	cattle	laughter	herd
Lucy	monkey		litter
Gir	elephants		
	lions		

Pages 36

Once upon a time, there lived a family of three bears in the woods. They were Mama Bear, Papa Bear and Baby Bear. One day, they went out for a walk. Mama Bear cooked up some delicious porridge before they left.

While they were gone, a little girl named Goldilocks walked by their house. She smelt the porridge and her tummy began to

Page 37

rumble. She went in and saw three bowls on the table. She ran towards them and took a spoonful of Papa Bear's porridge. But it was too hot. Then, she grabbed a spoonful of Mama Bear's porridge. But it was too cold. Finally, she tried Baby Bear's porridge. It was just right! She ate it all up hungrily.

After a while, she felt sleepy. She spotted Papa Bear's bed, but it was too hard. She lay down on Mama Bear's bed, but it was too soft. Finally, she tried Baby Bear's bed, which was just right. She jumped onto the bed and fell asleep in a jiffy!

Soon, the bears returned home. Baby Bear started crying when he saw his porridge bowl empty. "Somebody ate all my porridge!" he cried and ran to his room. And what did he see there? A strange little girl fast asleep on his bed! Baby bear screamed loudly. Goldilocks woke up. She was shocked to see three angry bears at the foot of the bed. She jumped out and ran away as fast as she could.

Page 38

Singing birds make us happy.

A camel is called the ship of the desert.

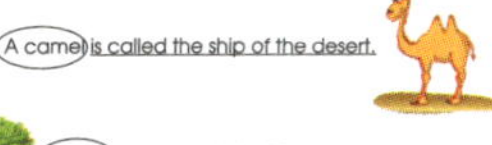

Forests have a variety of trees.

Cows give us milk.

Wild animals live in jungles.

Dogs are a man's best friend.

Page 39

A horse is the ______, whereas the mare is the female.
a. mail b. male

There are ______ many bees in this forest.
a. too b. two

We saw a ______ on our hiking trip.
a. deer b. dear

Did you ______ the sound of the bear?
a. here b. hear

The cat is ______ favourite pet.
a. their b. there

The ______ lost the race.
a. hair b. hare

Page 40

Once there was **a** cute little leopard,
But he didn't want to be cute,
He wanted to be **a** shepherd!

What he loved most was to keep
A close, watchful eye,
On those naughty little sheep.

He liked to watch them graze all day,
Then lead them back home
For **a** good night's stay.

But the sheep didn't like **the** leopard too much;
They were afraid of his sharp touch.

When they saw **the** leopard coming by,
They ran as fast
As their little feet could try.

The leopard was sad, but what could he do?
He gave up being **a** shepherd,
And went to **a** zoo!

Page 41

The hungry lion is (roaring).

The owl is (hiding) because it is daytime.

The crow is (flying) down to (steal) the cheese.

Goldilocks (fell asleep) on baby bear's bed.

The animals are (drinking) water from the stream.

Why is your dog (walking) like that?

She (took) her cat to the vet.

All his friends (thanked) the bear.

The crafty fox (hides) behind that bush every day.

A tiny mouse (lived) under the hole.

Page 42

The bird is flying high up in the sky.
present tense

I will take my dog for a walk shortly.
future tense

The boy saw how the elephant was being bathed.
past tense

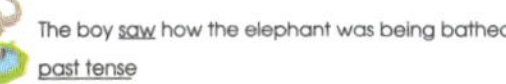

The cat rolled in the sand and got dirty.
past tense

My pet dog is drinking milk this morning.
present tense

Page 43

s	l	e	b	s	l	e	p	o	n	g
w	q	f	e	r	o	c	t	g	r	u
i	w	b	a	i	w	k	m	r	u	m
m	f	e	r	o	c	i	o	u	s	p
g	r	a	c	e	f	u	l	m	c	g
i	w	u	i	i	w	k	m	p	a	m
m	e	t	p	r	e	t	t	y	r	p
m	h	i	u	m	s	l	i	m	y	g
i	w	f	l	d	h	l	l	a	z	y
n	z	u	n	n	y	k	n	z	a	n
s	h	l	g	g	p	u	w	i	l	d

Circled: ferocious, graceful, beautiful, grumpy, scary, pretty, slimy, shy, lazy, wild

Page 44

The dog has two puppies.
adjective of quantity

The giraffe is a tall animal.
adjective of quality

The crafty fox wanted the cheese.
adjective of quality

Some birds cannot fly.
adjective of quantity

There are many species of animals, birds and insects to be found.
adjective of quantity

Elephants have long trunks.
adjective of quality

Dinosaurs are extinct animals.
adjective of quality

Page 45

Hyenas laugh **loudly**.

A cat can catch a mouse **easily**.

Cheetahs run **quickly**.

We **often** go trekking in the forest.

The little bird sang **joyfully**.

Page 46

If a cow is female, a male is a **bull**.

If a tigress is female, a male is a **tiger**.

If a lioness is female, a male is a **lion**.

If a mare is female, a male is a **stallion**.

If a hen is female, a male is a **rooster**.

Page 47

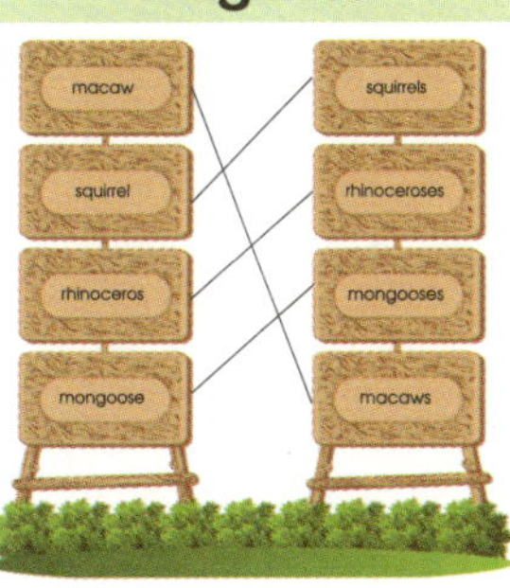

Page 48

This is a dense forest.

Wild beasts inhabit the forest.

Pretty flowers grow amidst the trees.

Our ecology needs to be preserved.

The berries that grow here are delicious.

A clear stream is flowing here.

The antelope has big horns.

crammed	S	clear	A
mild	A	untamed	S
beautiful	S	repulsive	A
destroyed	A	conserved	S
nasty	A	tasty	S
murky	A	clean	S
small	A	large	S

Page 49

(**I** / She) like animals.

Jack and (**I** / me) are watching a movie about bears.

(**That** / These) puppy needs water.

Dolly likes turtles. (**She** / He) has got one as a pet.

Mary told (**me** / I) an interesting story about elephants.

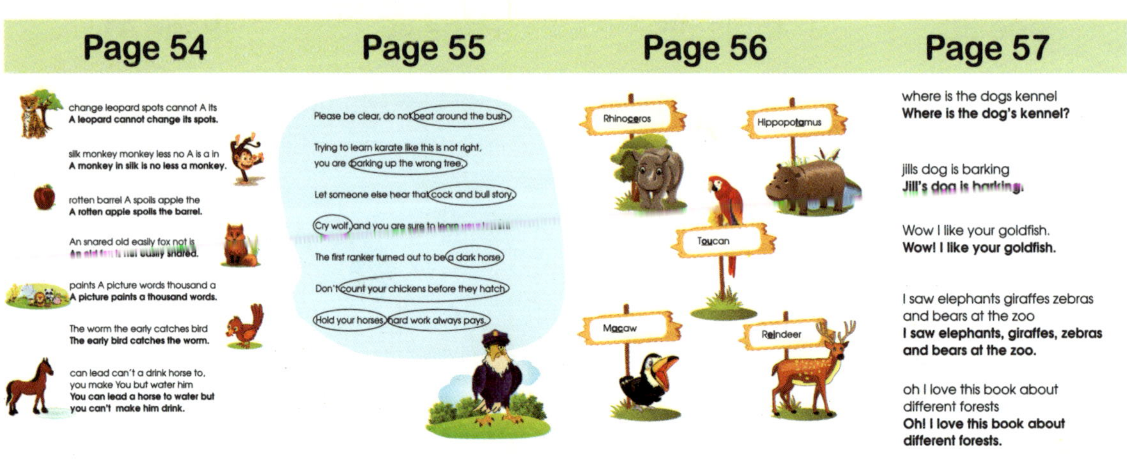

Pages 58-59

Answer the questions given below.

Which is the fastest animal on land?
Cheetah is the fastest animal on land.

Which family does the cheetah belong to?
Cheetah belongs to the cat family.

What sound does a cheetah make?
Cheetahs make a purring sound.

When do cheetahs hunt?
Cheetahs hunt mostly during the day, either late in the morning or early in the evening.

How do cheetahs move in different directions while running?
Cheetahs use their tail to steer in the right direction.

Page 63

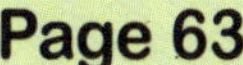

Page 64

kera
rake

kela
lake

ceak
cake

Page 65

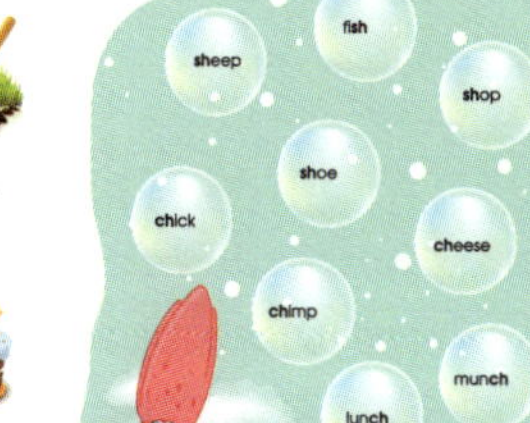

Page 66

Page 67

Page 68

Page 69

Page 70

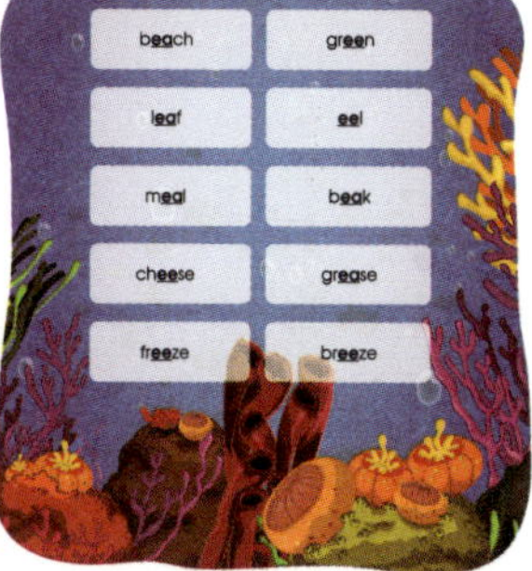

Page 71

Page 72

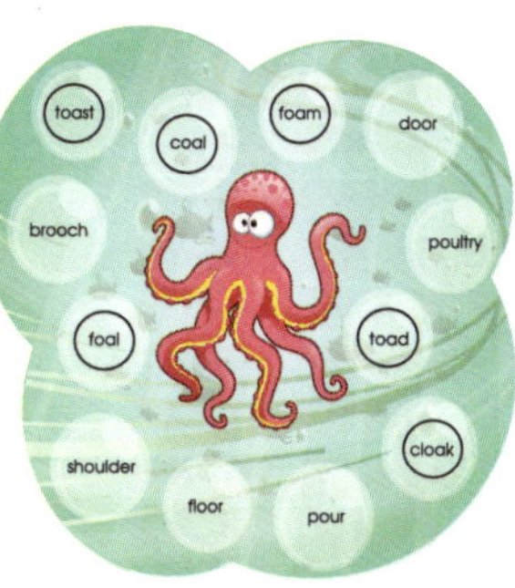

Page 73

Page 74

c	b	t	r	a	i	n	g
l	b	b	c	d	e	f	d
a	l	n	o	w	a	y	e
y	p	m	d	a	y	h	f
q	p	r	s	i	j	i	g
m	a	y	t	t	a	i	l
y	y	z	u	v	w	x	k
a	b	p	l	a	y	c	t
d	e	l	k	l	m	n	r
f	s	a	i	l	p	o	a
p	a	i	l	q	r	s	y
g	h	n	i	s	a	y	j

Page 75

The rabbit's **hair** is furry. (hare/hair)

Here are a **pair** of turtles. (pare/pair)

Help the octopus up these **stairs.** (stairs/stares)

The little jellyfish seems hurt and in **pain.** (pane/pain)

They call her a **plain** fish. (plane/plain)

The lion's **mane** is beautiful. (mane/main).

Page 76

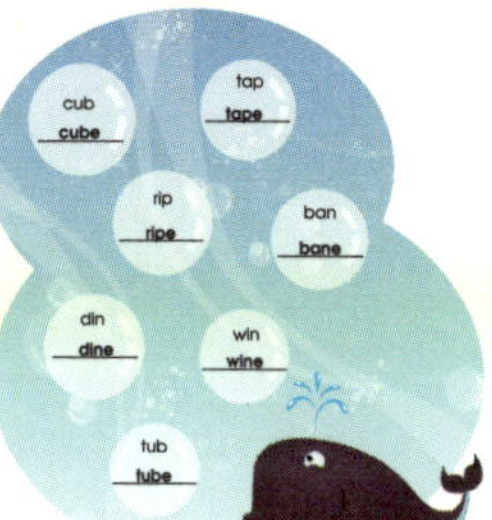

Page 77

cook
book
hoof
room
glue
prunes
broom
blue

Page 78

I ring in temples, I ring in churches,
I ring in your home and in palaces.
I am a **bell**.

My sides are round, I'm underground,
And within me, water can be found.
I am a **well**.

Supporting buildings, standing tall,
I'm made of bricks; I rhyme with fall.
I am a **wall**.

Hit me with a bat, or bounce me around,
I'm colourful and oh so round.
I am a **ball**.

Page 79

fish	belly
smile	myrtle
hill	jar
dress	mile
jelly	mess
star	bill
turtle	potter
otter	dish

Page 80

You **could** even take a cart.

You **should** not tell lies

I **would** help him myself if I were there.

Could you look after my fish please?

Would you please sit down!

We **should** preserve marine life.

Page 81

I **think** I will learn to swim.

That was a nice cake.

This is a nice lake.

What's that roaring noise in the sky? It's **thunder**.

The river **Thames** flows through London city.

The Ganges is a sacred river in India.

Thank you! I appreciate your kindness.

Trains were not working. **Therefore**, we took the bus.

the this that think

thunder therefore thames thank

Page 82

scene breathe lean sheath teen green beneath teethe clean wean

mean wreath

Page 83 Page 84 Page 85 Page 86

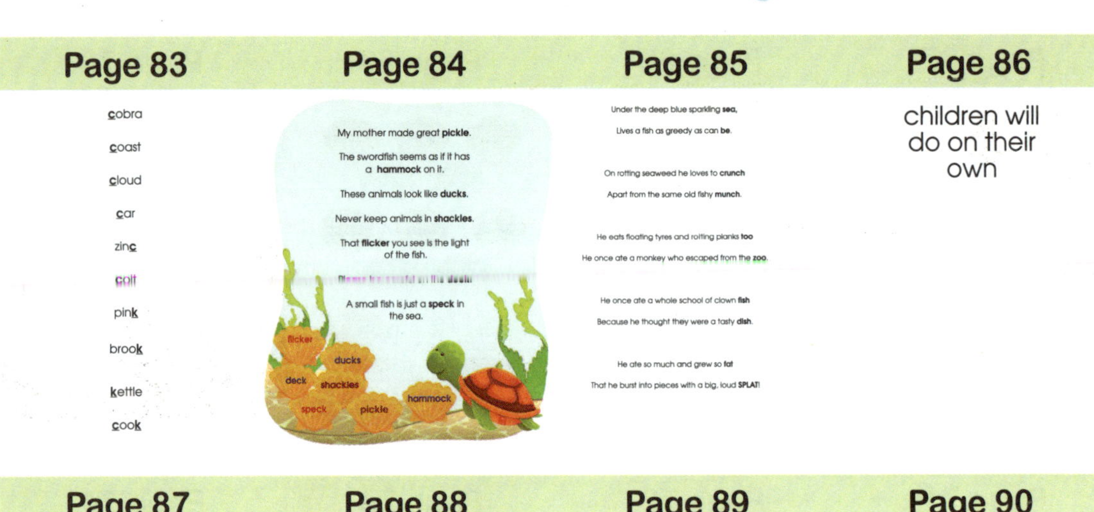

Page 87 Page 88 Page 89 Page 90

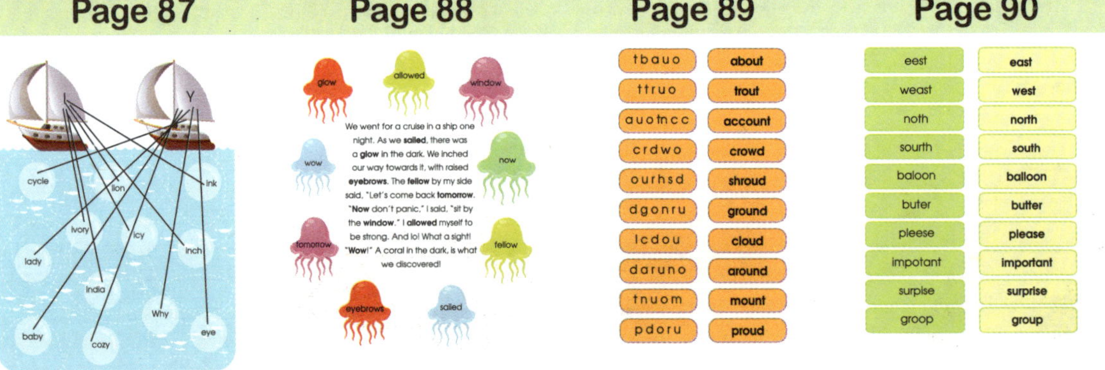

Page 91

children will do on their own

Page 123

101	111	121	131	141	151	161	171	181	191
102	112	122	132	142	152	162	172	182	192
103	113	123	133	143	153	163	173	183	193
104	114	124	134	144	154	164	174	184	194
105	115	125	135	145	155	165	175	185	195
106	116	126	136	146	156	166	176	186	196
107	117	127	137	147	157	167	177	187	197
108	118	128	138	148	158	168	178	188	198
109	119	129	139	149	159	169	179	189	199
110	120	130	140	150	160	170	180	190	200

Page 124

Circle

Triangle

Square

Pentagon

Rectangle

Star

Heart

Diamond

Page 125

101	One hundred and one
115	One hundred and fifteen
120	One hundred and twenty
129	One hundred and twenty-nine
133	One hundred and thirty-three
141	One hundred and forty-one
148	One hundred and forty-eight
150	One hundred and fifty

Page 126

I can see 10 space shuttles.

I can see 8 planets.

I can see 9 comets.

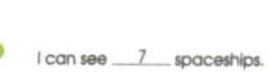

I can see 7 spaceships.

Page 127

13 + 30 = 43

57 + 22 = 79

74 + 19 = 93

62 + 34 = 96

19 + 54 = 73

51 + 35 = 86

Page 128

9 – 3 = 6

15 – 7 = 8

20 – 8 = 12

31 – 9 = 22

39 – 4 = 35

19 – 9 = 10

26 – 10 = 16

42 – 16 = 26

Page 129

Page 130-131

Six tens and five ones – **65**

Three tens and seven ones – **37**

One ten and three ones – **13**

Nine tens and eight ones – **98**

Four tens and one one – **41**

Eight tens and two ones – **82**

Five tens and three ones – **53**

Two tens and two ones – **22**

Seven tens and four ones – **74**

Nine tens and zero ones – **90**

Zero tens and nine ones – **09**

Page 132

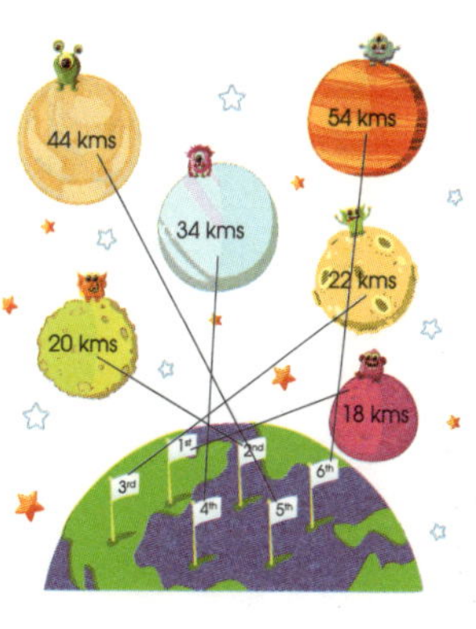

Page 133

Page 134

Page 135

Page 136

Page 137

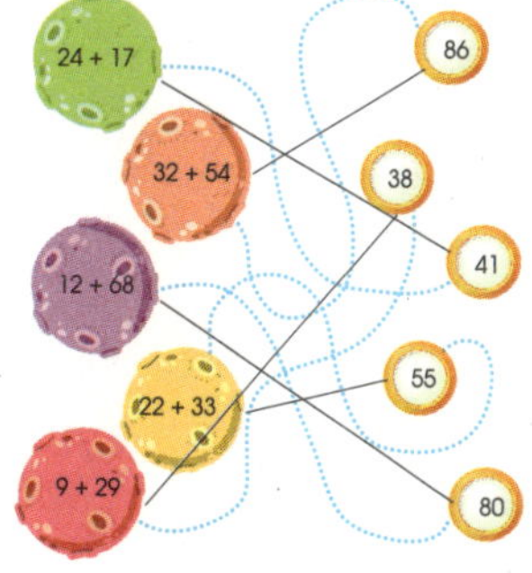

Page 138

Page 139

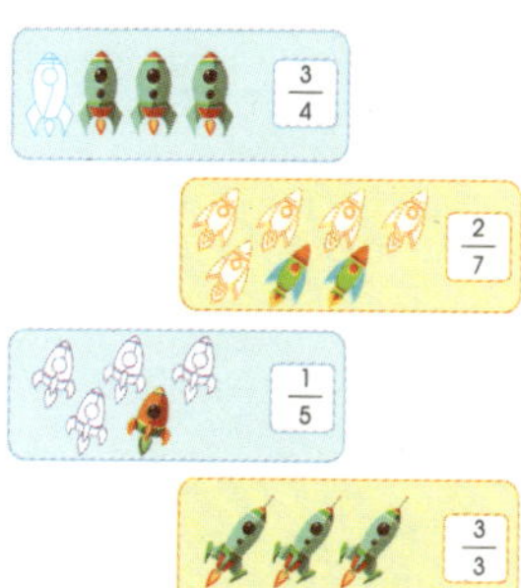

Page 140 | Page 141 | Page 142 | Page 143

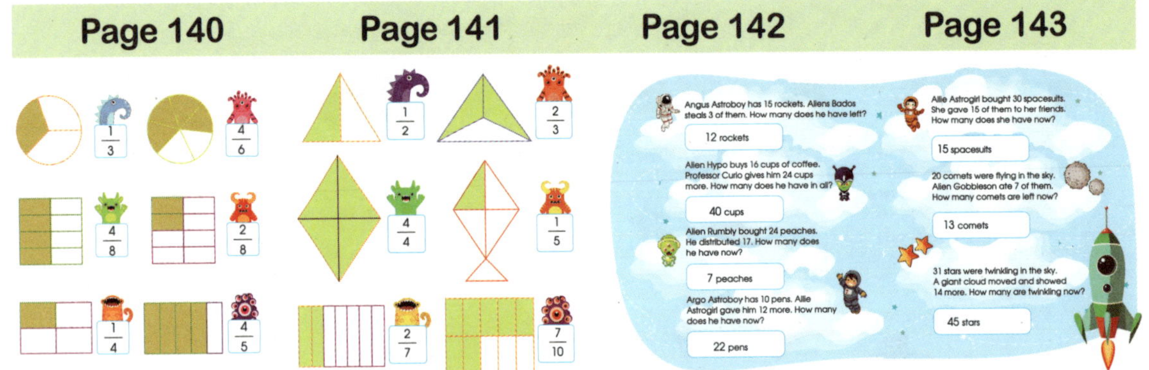

Page 144 | Page 145 | Page 146 | Page 147

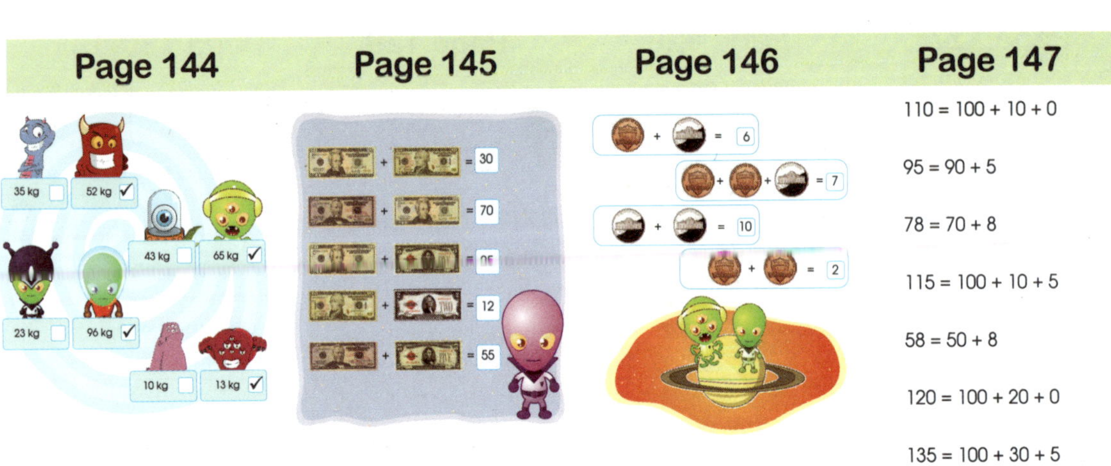

110 = 100 + 10 + 0

95 = 90 + 5

78 = 70 + 8

115 = 100 + 10 + 5

58 = 50 + 8

120 = 100 + 20 + 0

135 = 100 + 30 + 5

Page 148 | Page 149 | Page 150 | Page 151

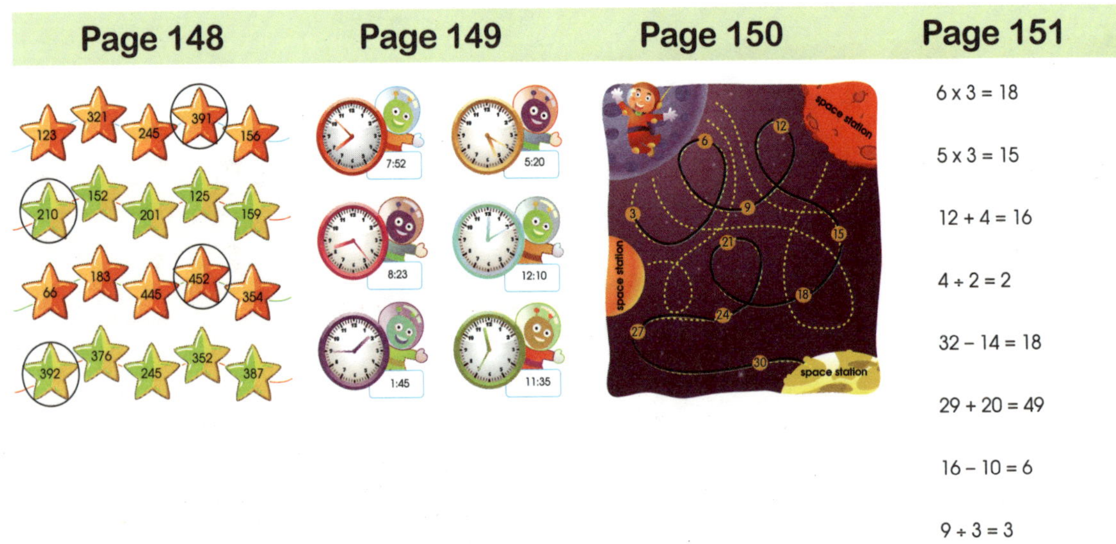

6 x 3 = 18

5 x 3 = 15

12 + 4 = 16

4 ÷ 2 = 2

32 – 14 = 18

29 + 20 = 49

16 – 10 = 6

9 ÷ 3 = 3

Page 152

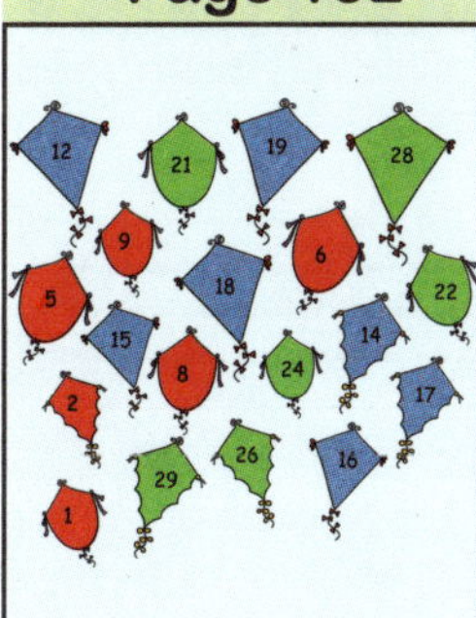

Page 153

Page 154

Page 155

Page 156

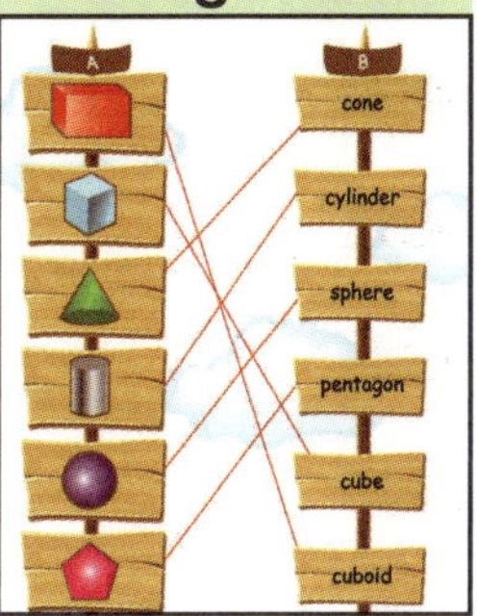

Page 157

Page 158

Page 159

Page 160

Page 161

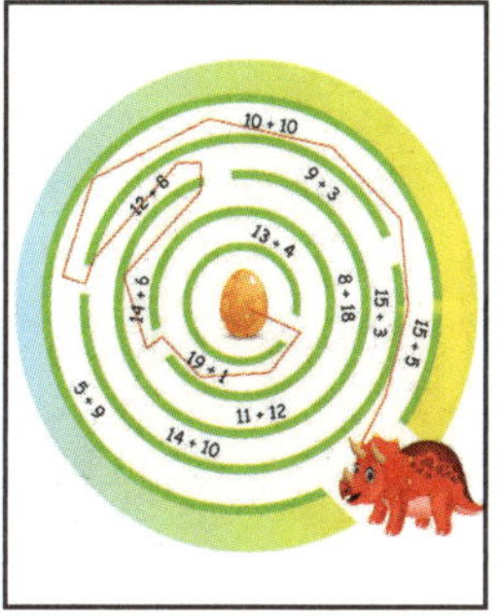

Page 162

Answer the following:

1. How many clothes did the Mathesaur find? 20
2. How many red and pink t-shirts did he find? 5
3. How many orange and green t-shirts did he find altogether? 5

Page 163

Page 164

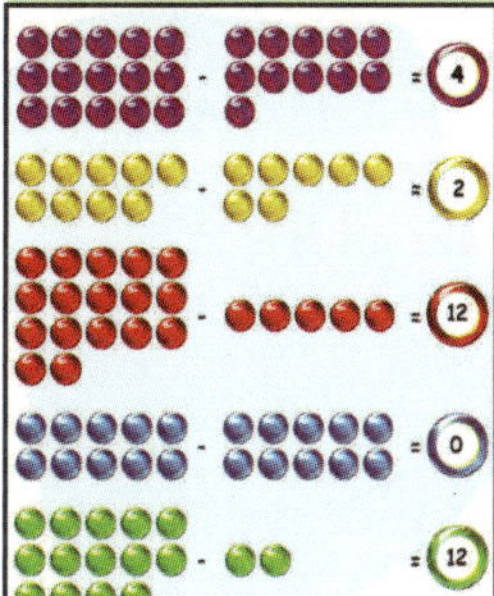

Page 165

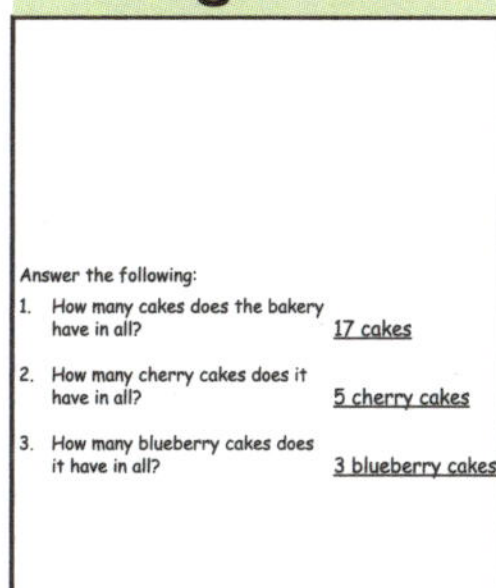

Page 166

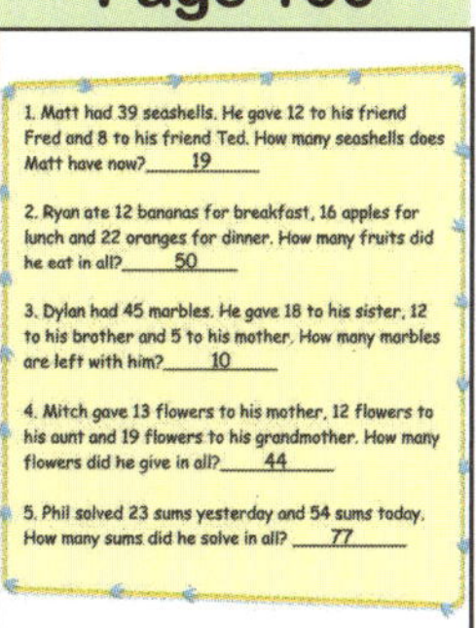

Page 167

Page 168

Page 169

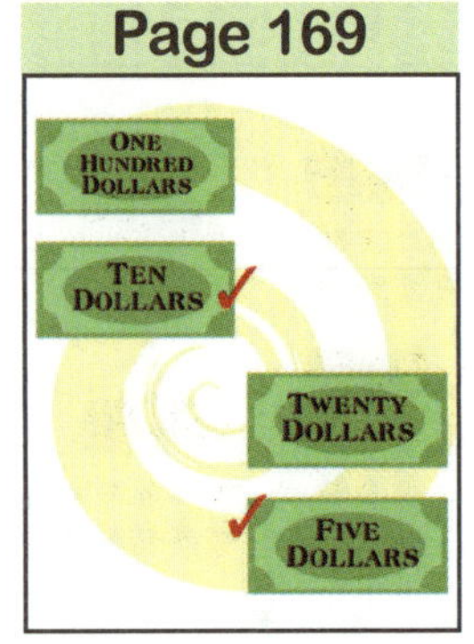

Page 170

Page 171

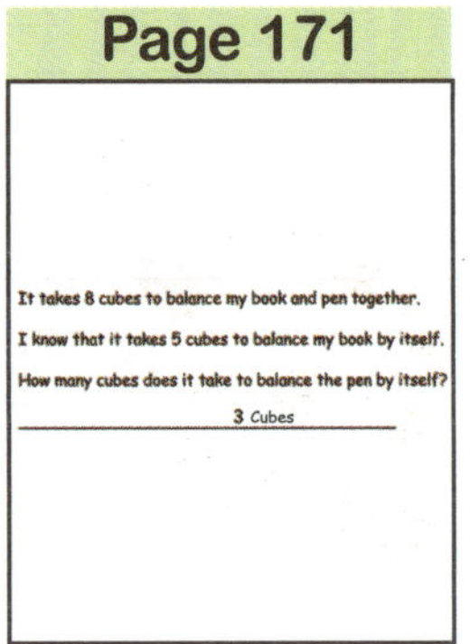

It takes 8 cubes to balance my book and pen together.

I know that it takes 5 cubes to balance my book by itself.

How many cubes does it take to balance the pen by itself?

3 Cubes

Page 172

Page 173

Page 174

Page 175

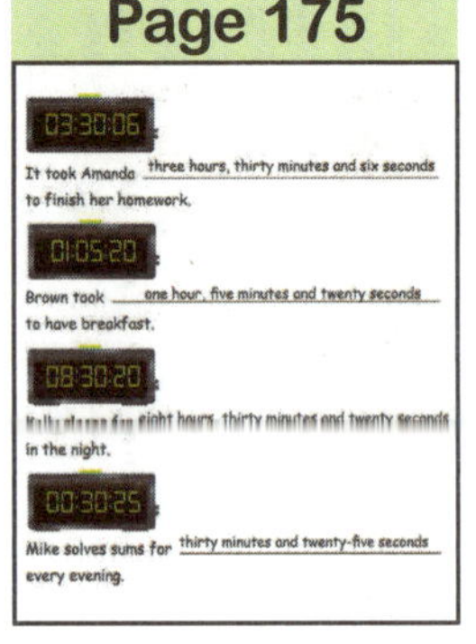

Page 176

Page 177

Page 178

Page 179

Page 180

Page 181

a. 17, c. 12, d. 20, e. 16, f. 12, g. 20, h. 12,

i. 14, j. 16, k. 10 l. 13, m. 10, n. 10, o. 15, p. 9,

q. 12, r. 11, s. 16, t. 17

Page 182

a. 29, b. 59, c. 89, d. 45 e. 59, f. 66, g. 77,

h. 63 i. 97, j. 98, k. 78, l. 78

Page 183

a. 82, b. 102, c. 121, d. 42

Students to write expanded form on their own.

Page 184

1. 9
2. Poppy, Emma, Pam
3. Poppy, Emma, Pam
4. Ronny
5. Apples and pears

Page 185

Pastime	Number of children
painting	4
reading	1
skating	3
cooking	3
playing football	2

Painting is most popular among Neo's friends.

Page 186

1. 20
2. 6
3. Social Science
4. Science
5. Writing

Page 187

Correct tally chart is:

Student	Tally count
Kate	𝍸 𝍸 𝍸 𝍸 𝍸 𝍸 II
Joy	𝍸 𝍸 𝍸 𝍸 III
Lilly	𝍸 𝍸 𝍸 𝍸 IIII
Suzie	𝍸 𝍸 𝍸 𝍸 𝍸 II
Jill	𝍸 𝍸 𝍸

- We hope Kate to win the quiz.
- 5 things that we know from the tally chart:

1. Five students participated in the quiz.
2. Kate has scored the highest.
3. Jill has scored the lowest.
4. Suzie scored more than Joy.
5. Lily is 1 point ahead of Joy.

Page 190

1. Snow white and the Seven Dwarfs
2. Cinderella
3. Cinderella- 1000, Peter Pan- 1220, Beauty and the Beast- 1300, Rapunzel- 1560, Pinocchio- 2000,
4. Snow White and Seven Dwarfs- 2380

Page 189

Sea creature	Tally count
Turtle	𝍸 II
Fish	𝍸 𝍸
Starfish	𝍸 III
Crab	𝍸 IIII
Jelly Fish	III
Eel	𝍸 II
Angelfish	𝍸 I
Sea Horse	𝍸 𝍸 I
Shark	I

1. angelfish- 6 turtle - 7 shark 1
   crab- 9 jelly fish- 3 starfish- 8
2. sea horse
3. 2
4. She saw 9 creatures to a count of 62

Page 191

1. France
2. Bangkok and France
3. Italy, Australia, Singapore
4. 18, 10, 9

Page 195

Piece of clothing	Frequency
Trousers	21
Shirt	10
Skirt	11
Shorts	19
Dress	15

1. Trousers- 21 Shirts- 10 Skirts- 11
   Dresses- 15 Shorts-19
2. 3 for boys, 2 for girls
3. 76
4. By adding all the frequencies or tally counts

Page 192

Ants	●●●●
Caterpillars	●●●
Butterflies	●●●●
Bees	●●●●
Ladybirds	●●●●●●●●●
Beetles	●

ants- 4 caterpillars- 3
butterflies- 4 bees- 4
ladybirds- 9 beetles- 1

Page 194

Children will make the pictogram on their own.
How many of each instrument does Mr Roger have?
violin- 8 drum -2 guitar-6
trumpet- 5 piano- 2

Page 196

Remote control car- 5 skates- 8
chocolates- 2 Board game- 10
water colours- 6 board game- 3
dress- 2 soft toy- 9 robot- 7

Page 197

Children will make pictogram on their own.

Page 198

Children will make pictogram on their own.

Page 200

1. dog- 7, cat- 9, fish- 3, guinea pig- 6, turtle- 5
2. cat
3. Fish

Page 201

1. Clown- 7, pirate- 3, sailor- 2, prince- 4, princess- 5, magician- 6
2. Clown
3. Sailor

Page 202

1. January- 7 degrees, April- 8 degrees, June- 15 degrees, August- 18 degrees, October- 14 degrees, December- 9 degrees
2. August
3. February
4. 18-7= 11 degrees

Page 203

1. Favourite snacks
2. Snack name
3. Burgers, French fries, Noodles, Cheese puff, Corn chips
4. Number of people
5. 0 15

Page 204

Children will draw the bar chart on their own.

Page 205

Subject	Number of books
Drawing	10
Physical Education	4
Painting	7
Creation	8
Geography	5
Maths	14
Geometry	11

Page 207

Cookies	Number of boxes ordered
Orange Cookies	10
Choco chip cookies	8
Orange cookies	12
Strawberry cookies	9
Salty cookies	5
Oats cookies	6
Cashew cookies	15

Page 210

1. Strawberry-13, vanilla- 11, both- 3 only strawberry- 10, only vanilla- 8
2. Ronny asked 21 friends.

Page 211

Children will make venn diagram on their own.

Page 212

3 – rectangle
4 – square
5 – hexagon
6 – triangle
7 – rectangle
8 – octagon
9 – square
10 – pentagon

Page 213

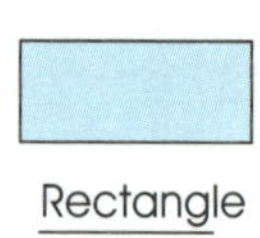
Rectangle

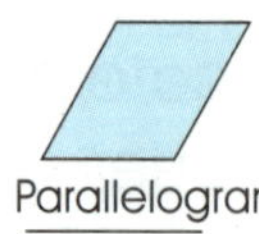
Parallelogram

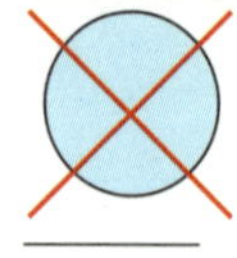

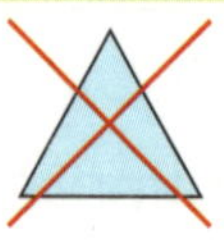

Square

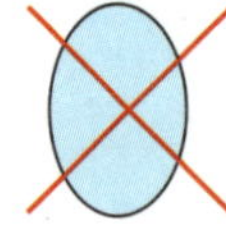

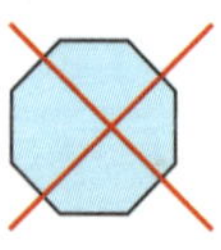

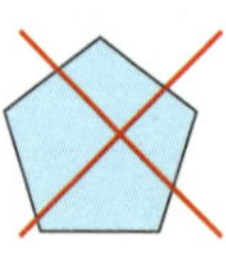

Page 214

play

celebrate festivals

read and study

go on a picnic

Page 215

1. False
2. True
3. True
4. True
5. True
6. True
7. True
8. true

Page 216

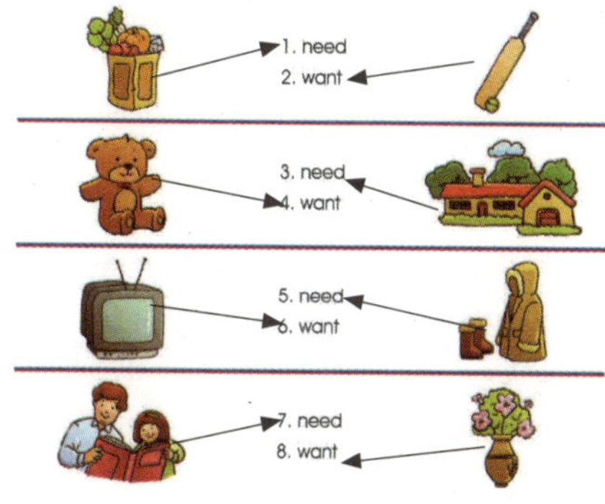

Page 217

1. cleaner's shop, grocery store, bus stop, hardware shop
2. Sterling Apartments
3. France Groceries
4. park
5. city

Page 218

Children will do on their own.
Answers will vary.

Page 219

Children will do on their own.

Page 220

Page 221

1. Library
2. Fire Department
3. Police
4. Park's Office
5. Ambulance
6. Post Office
7. Water Services
8. Garbage Collection
9. Animal Control
10. Power Company

Page 222

1. agree
2. agree
3. disagree
4. agree
5. disagree

6 agree

7. disagree
8. disagree
9. disagree
10. disagree

Page 223

1. The driver of the yellow car.
2. The driver of the yellow car has skipped the red light.
3. The policeman should stop and warn him for breaking rules.

Page 224

Page 226

1. One
2. Read books
3. Newspaper
4. Sign board
5. Danger! No swimming

Page 227

1. Post office
2. E-mails
3. Telephone
4. Mobile phones
5. Television
6. Book
7. Newspaper

Page 228

1. False- Thousands of years ago, man used to travel from one place to another using carts, animals.
2. False- In rural areas, people usually travel by carts, other small vehicles.
3. False- Horses were used to pull carts some years ago
4. False- Things like coal, vehicles and goods are transported by goods trains.
5. False- The fastest means of transportation is aeroplane.
6. False- A submarine remains inside the water.
7. False- Trains run on steel tracks that are called tracks.
8. False- A helicopter can carry less number of people.

Page 230

Map A is Kate's neighbourhood.

Page 231

1. Mom's room
2. Ron
3. Kim
4. Children will circle on their own.
5. Seven

Page 232

1. South, east, west
2. North
3. East
4. South
5. West

Page 233

1. Monkey house
2. Tiger house
3. Elephant house
4. Two
5. Lion house would be to the left and no house on the right

Page 234

1. West
2. South
3. North
4. East

Page 235

1.  

2. A house

3.

4. One

5. 

Page 236

1. 

2. 

3. five

4. Elm Street, Main Street, Oak Street, Maple Street

5. Children will circle the post office on their own

Page 237

1. Irish Sea, Celtic Sea
2. North
3. East
4. Children will draw symbols on their own.
5. There are three rivers.

Page 239

1. Island
2. Lake
3. Plain
4. River
5. Peninsula

Page 240

water, fruits, soil, wool and wood are natural resources

Page 241

These are ways to take care of natural resources:

- Throw litter in the trash can
- Use things again
- Take care of birds and animals
- Help to keep the surroundings clean

Page 243

Children will do on their own.

Page 246

Across:	Down:
2 coat	1. parts
5. different	3. light
8. embryo	4. protects
10. sprout	6. food
12. eat	7. coconut
13. water	9. travel
14. wind	11. food

Page 247

True statements

Roots: 1. Fix the plant in the soil. 2. Some roots like carrot, turnip, radish and beetroot store food in them.	**Stem:** 1. Gives support to the plants. 2. Carries water and nutrients from the roots to the leaves. 3. Leaves, flowers, buds and fruits grow on the stem.
Leaves: 1. Help the plant breathe. 2. Store food.	**Flowers:** 1. Make seeds. 2. Attract insects and birds. 3. Store food.

Page 247

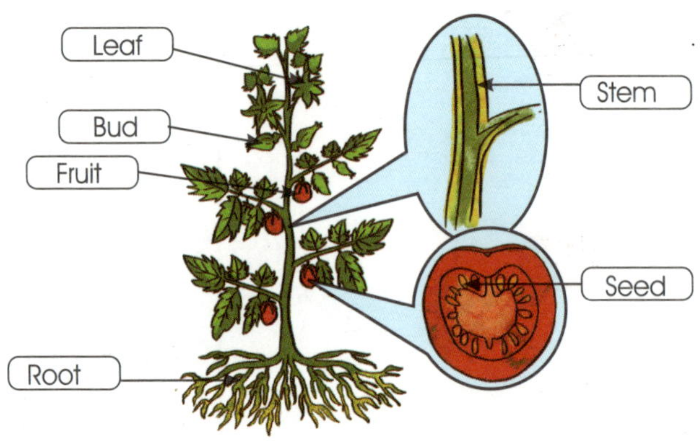

Page 249

1. cotton
2. mint
3. coconut
4. watermelon
5. pea

Page 251

Rose - thorns
Cactus - spikes
Touch me not plant - closes its leaves when touched
Lotus - waxy leaves to help it float on water
Poison ivy - produces an oil to protect itself

Page 253

Life cycle of butterfly:
eggs, caterpillar, pupa, butterfly
Fill in the blanks:

1. leaf
2. larva

3. caterpillar
4. skin
5. two, butterfly

section 3:

sting and bite

colours and body

bad

Page 255

eggs, spiderlings, hatch, backs, spiderlings, spin, prey, autumn

Page 256

Reptiles:

chameleon, alligator, iguana, snake, crocodile, tortoise, lizard

True/false:

1. False
2. True
3. True
4. False
5. True

Page 257:

Snakes:

- Have no legs
- Have a strong sense of smell
- Shed their skin
- Poison , fangs

Lizards:

- crawling
- bugs, insects, small creatures
- shedding their tail

Tortoises:

- shell
- land
- plants
- head and limbs

Page 258

1. jelly
2. gills
3. legs
4. froglet
5. frog

Page 259

1. feathers
2. wings
3. strong
4. boat shaped
5. beak
6. hollow, fly

Page 260

1. Long slender beak
2. Hooked beak
3. Slender curved beak
4. Spatulate beak
5. Small conical beak
6. Slender beak
7. Sharp beak
8. Short curved and downward-facing beak
9. Long slender beak
10. Spatulate beak

Page 261

1. elephant
2. dolphin
3. dog
4. bear
5. giraffe

Page 264

1. scales
2. protect
3. gills
4. membranes, breathe
5. steer, balance
6. tail

Page 265

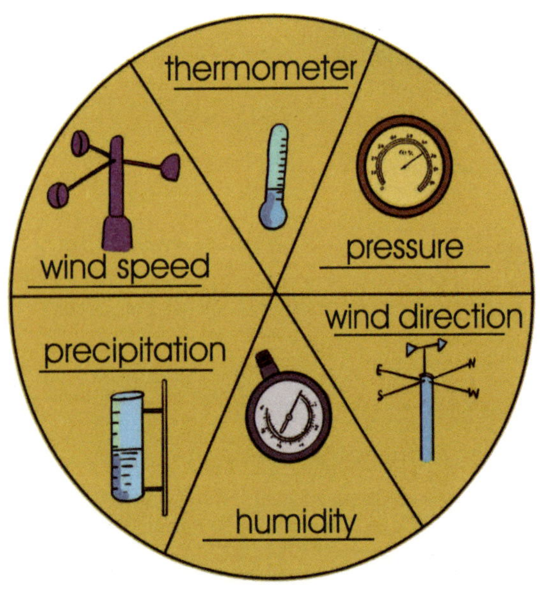

wind vane, thermometer, rain gauge

Page 266

temperature: hot, thermometer, hotter

wind: moving, warms, rises, cool, wind

humidity: moisture, oceans, heated, water vapour

air pressure: weight

Page 268

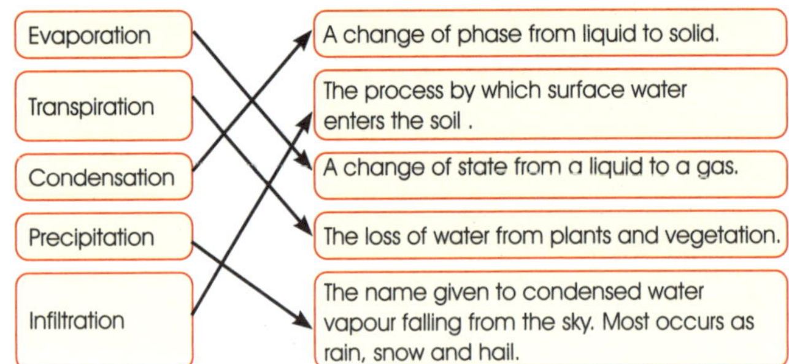

Page 270

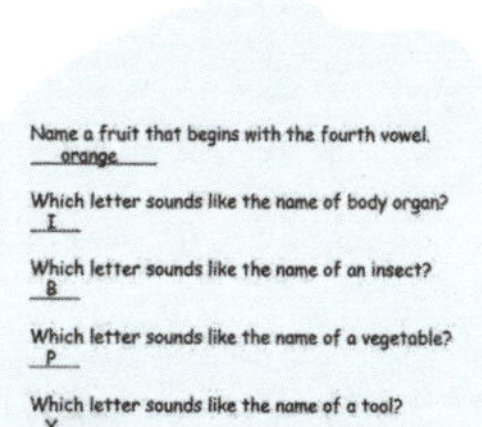
Name a fruit that begins with the fourth vowel. orange
Which letter sounds like the name of body organ? I
Which letter sounds like the name of an insect? B
Which letter sounds like the name of a vegetable? P
Which letter sounds like the name of a tool? X
Which letter sounds like the name given to a group of people standing in a line? Q

Page 271

I walk on sand in the desert. c a m e l
I am a vegetable that makes you cry. o n i o n
I tell you what time it is. c l o c k
I give you a lot of wool. s h e e p
I am a red fruit. a p p l e
You write with me on a blackboard. c h a l k

Page 272

I saw grapes (persga) growing on a vine (ivne).
Their bunches (esnbuhc) are looking beautiful and nice.
Some are green (negre) and some are black (acblk).
Some are sweet (teswe) and some are sour (rous).
Children love to eat (tea) them more.

Page 273

For this activity, the answers will vary.

Page 274

Page 275

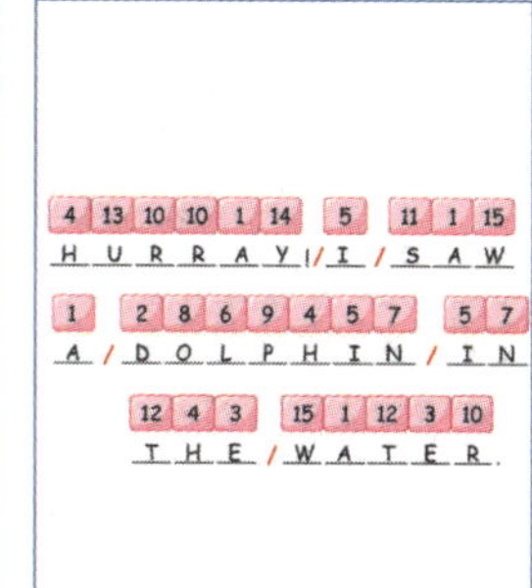

Page 276

Page 277

Give me a slice of cake.
Give me a bunch of grapes.
Give me a pack of biscuits.
Give me a cup of tea.
Give me a glass of milk.
Give me a basket of fruits.
Give me a scoop of ice cream.

Page 278

For this activity, the answers will vary.

Page 279

For this activity, the answers will vary.

Page 280

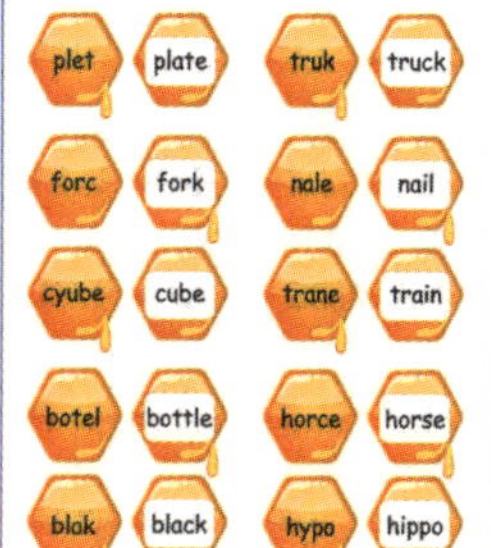

Page 281

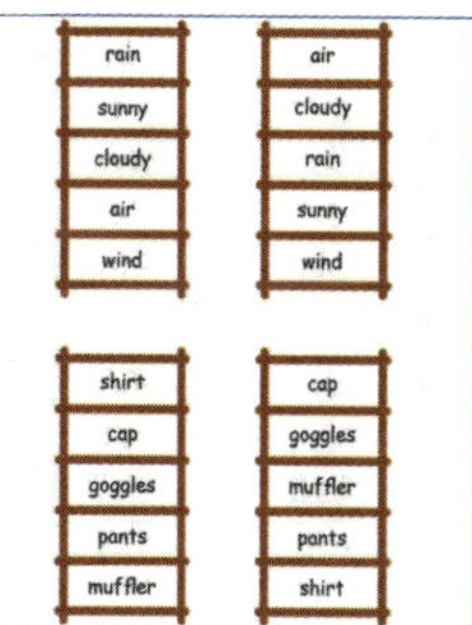

Page 282

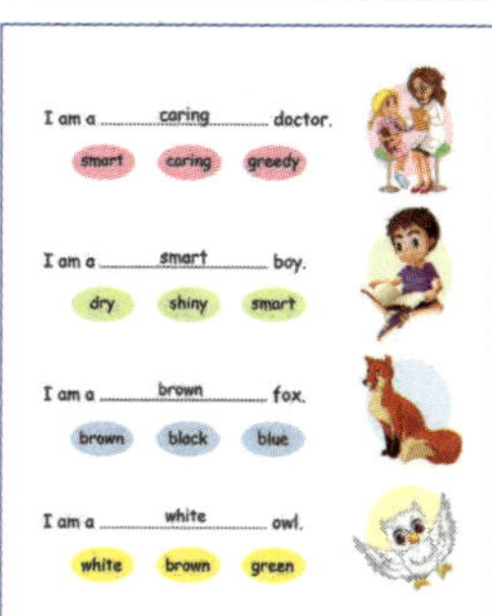
I am a caring doctor. smart caring greedy
I am a smart boy. dry shiny smart
I am a brown fox. brown black blue
I am a white owl. white brown green

Page 283

I am a big animal. big small tiny
I am a brave soldier. brave smart scared
I am a pretty girl. pretty big soft
I am a colourful bird. black colourful white
I am a tall animal. short round tall

Page 284

Page 285

He is crying
He is happy
He is sad
He is angry
He is scared
He is laughing

Page 286

Page 287

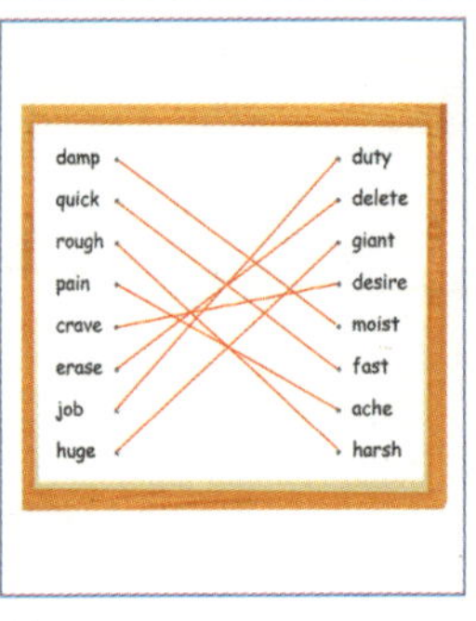

Page 288

Page 289

Page 290

Page 291

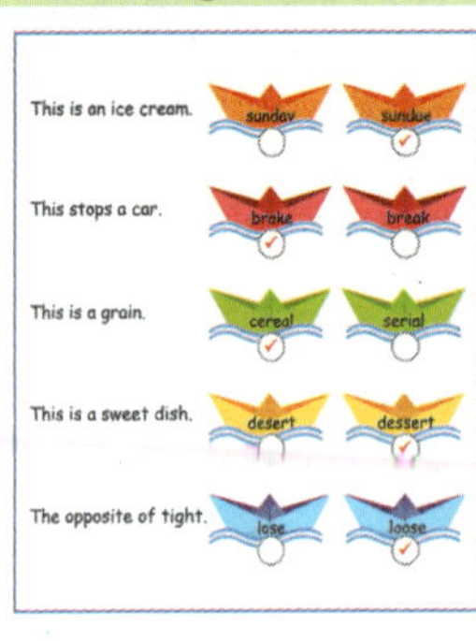

Page 292

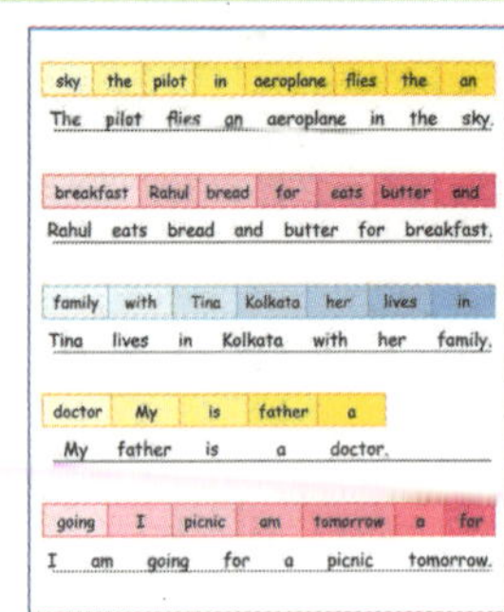

Page 293

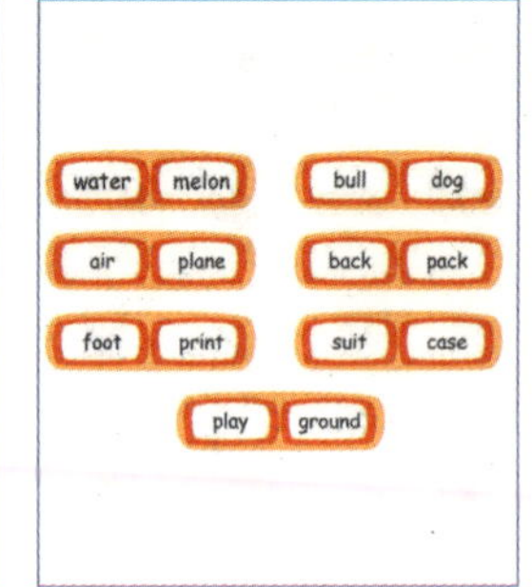

Page 294

Page 295

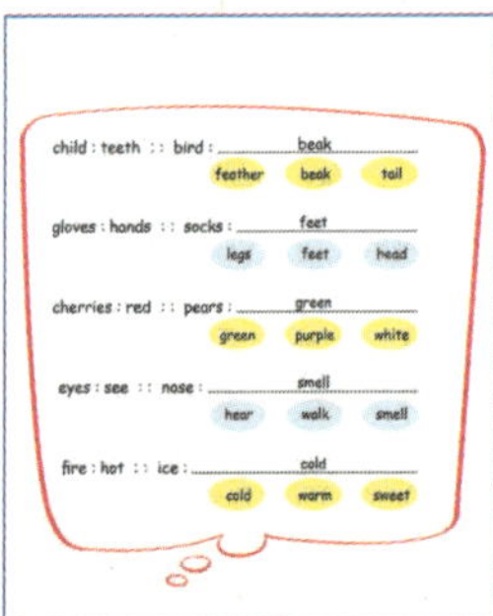

Page 296

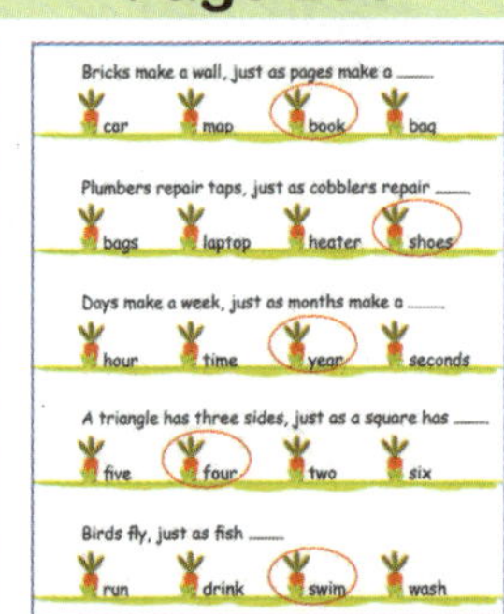

Page 297

Page 298

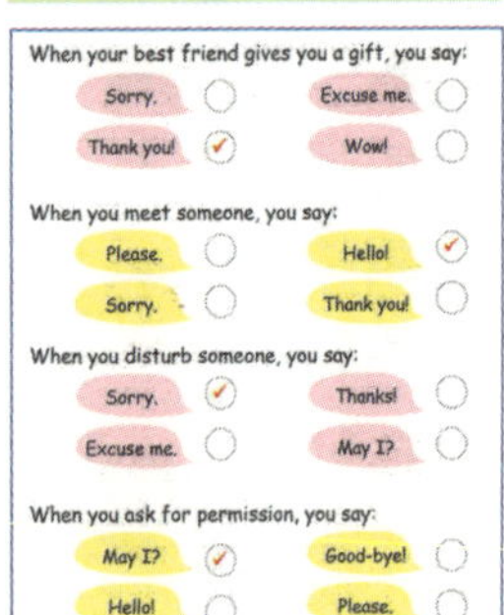